JAMIE MADIGAN, PHD

THE PSYCHOLOGY OF DUNGEONS & DRAGONS

HOW TO BE A BETTER, MORE ENGAGED, AND HAPPIER PLAYER OR GAME MASTER

Leyline Publishing, Inc.
Fort Worth, TX

All rights reserved. No part of this book may be used or reproduced in any manner whatsoever without prior written permission, except for brief quotation of less than one hundred (100) words for reviews and articles.

Leyline Publishing, Inc.

7801 Oakmont Blvd, Suite 101
Fort Worth, Texas 76132
www.leylinepublishing.com | https://geektherapeutics.com

Printed in the United States of America
10 9 8 7 6 5 4 3 2 1

Library of Congress Cataloging-in-Publication Data is available upon request.
Paperback ISBN: 978-1-955406-27-7
Digital ISBN: 978-1-955406-28-4

Editing by Anthony M. Bean
Copyediting and Proofreading by Madeline Jones
Text Design and composition by Asya Blue
Cover Design and Illustration by Sam Rusk

THE PSYCHOLOGY OF
DUNGEONS
& DRAGONS

DEDICATION

For all the folks I've rolled d20s with in the last decade: Allen, Bill, Cameron, Dave, Eric, George, Jason, Joe, Kevin, Mark, Matt, Mercedes, Mitch, Patrick, Paul, other Paul, and Pete. And special thanks to Sam, who provided so much thoughtful advice and feedback on this book.

CONTENTS

INTRODUCTION | 1

PART I
Why We Play | 5

CHAPTER 1
Why Do We Feel So
Heroic While Playing
Dungeons & Dragons? | 7

CHAPTER 2
Why Is the Open-Ended Freedom
of *Dungeons & Dragons* So Appealing? | 23

CHAPTER 3
Why Do We Love Feeling Important to
Both Real and Imaginary People? | 37

CHAPTER 4
How Does *Dungeons & Dragons* Pull Us
into Imaginary Worlds? | 51

CHAPTER 5
Why Do Some Players Hoard Stuff Like
They're Dragons? | 67

PART II
Playing The Game | 79

CHAPTER 6
Why and How Do We Identify with Our
In-Game Characters? | 81

CHAPTER 7
What Gets Us to Role-Play and Why Should We Care? | 95

CHAPTER 8
How Do Players Judge Alignment and Morality? | 111

CHAPTER 9
What Do We Get Wrong About Unlucky
Dice and Natural 20s? | 127

CHAPTER 10
How Do We Deal with So Many In-Game Choices? | 145

PART III
Party Dynamics | 163

CHAPTER 11
When Do Players Work Together Best? | 165

CHAPTER 12
Which is Better: Playing In-Person or Online? | 181

CHAPTER 13
Does Creating a Game World Make It
More Fun to Play In? | 197

CHAPTER 14
Why Do We Escape into Imaginary Worlds? | 211

CHAPTER 15
Does Playing *Dungeons & Dragons*
Turn Kids into Devil Worshipers? | 225

CHAPTER 16
Does Playing *Dungeons & Dragons* Help Us Improve
Our Skills and Mental Health? | 227

CONCLUSION | 241

GLOSSARY | 243

REFERENCES | 247

ENDNOTES | 257

ABOUT THE AUTHOR

Jamie Madigan, PhD has become an expert on the psychology of games and seeks to popularize understanding of how various research from the psychology literature can be used to understand why games are designed the way they are and why players behave as they do. Dr. Madigan has written extensively on the subject for various magazines, websites, books, and his own site at www.psychologyofgames.com. He has also spoken at conferences about the intersection of psychology and games. Finally, he has appeared as an expert on the psychology of games in dozens of print, radio, podcast, and web outlets such as Good Morning America, The Washington Post, the Chicago Tribune, BBC Radio 5, the BBC, The Guardian, and more. He has played *Dungeons & Dragons* since the early 1980s which, according to three different calendars he referenced, is a long time.

INTRODUCTION

To say that *Dungeons & Dragons* is having a moment wouldn't do justice to its burst of popularity in the last decade. The game, which lets friends engage in rules-bound storytelling in a fantasy setting with the help of the occasional die roll, had modest beginnings in the 1970s and then became a cultural touchstone during the 1980s. Today, it's more popular than ever thanks to an accessible new edition, online tools, a ceaseless stream of new books, and a growing number of people playing it for audiences online. Despite its nerdy roots, the game has gone mainstream with tie-in products for TV hits like *Big Bang Theory*, *Rick and Morty*, *Stranger Things*, and others. A Dungeons & Dragons movie starring Hugh Grant and Chris Pine came out in 2023 and multiple television shows are in the works as I write this. The mega-popular YouTube show *Critical Role* draws record-bursting audiences who watch professional actors play *Dungeons & Dragons*. The single, three-hour episode I'm looking at right now has 13 million views. If that's not all enough proof for you, consider that the fast-food restaurant Arby's released a set of official *Dungeons & Dragons* dice, and rival restaurant Wendy's put out an adventure where you fight Ronald McDonald at the end.

With this level of popularity and cultural cachet, you might be curious about how the game affects us and what goes on in our minds when we play. That's where this book comes in. It will help you enjoy the game more, run it more smoothly, get along better with your fellow players, and approach play on your own terms. It will do this by explaining how the psychology behind the game drives how we play the game, how we form relationships with other players, and how we change once we put away the dice and step away from the table. For example, what is it about playing tabletop role-playing games (TTRPGs) like *Dungeons & Dragons* that appeals to our basic psychological needs in ways that other activities and even other kinds of games can't? What kinds of mental skills are needed to engage in role-playing where you take on the perspective of fictional characters? How do we tend to think incorrectly about lucky (or unlucky) die rolls and critical hits? What kinds of psychological short-cuts come into play when dealing with what seems like overwhelming choices inherent to playing the game? Is playing *Dungeons & Dragons* online as satisfying and mentally healthy as playing it in person? How can playing the game help us escape the stress of everyday life and develop useful skills?

I'll cover all those questions and more, with a particular eye on what scientific research from psychology and neighboring fields has to provide in terms of answers. And we won't just be exploring one part of the vast and varied field which is psychology. We'll touch on the parts that you may be familiar with, such as the use of *Dungeons & Dragons* for mental health therapy, but we'll also venture into other corners of the field that deal with the psychology of social interactions, personality, work in organizations, learning, media, decision-making, and more.

It's important to note that this isn't a textbook. It's neither structured like one nor written like one. You don't need a degree in psychology or even any prior knowledge of the field in order to follow along. Instead, this book is meant to be a practical guide for players and game masters who are at least a little bit curious about the intersection of their favorite game and the field of psychology. Each chapter contains practical tips and takeaways for everyone at the table to use when prepping for, thinking about, and playing their games. The objective is to give you tips and insights that you can use, so much so that each chapter will conclude with a convenient list of everything you learned and specific

INTRODUCTION

ways you can apply it to your games. It's also worth pointing out that while I mostly refer to *Dungeons & Dragons* because it's the game I know best and it's currently the most popular role-playing game on the market, the advice and information in these pages are largely applicable to any kind of TTRPG. In almost every case you can easily apply what's here to other game systems or even to designing your own systems. It is as useful to game designers as it is to players.

That all said, while this book assumes that you're familiar with *Dungeons & Dragons* to at least a passing degree, you don't need to be an expert. You don't need to have been the game master in an epic campaign or played since you were old enough not to choke on the dice. If you need it, many great primers on the game are just a web search away, including ones from the game's publisher, Wizards of the Coast. None of them would take long to teach you what you need. So for the sake of this book's flow and readability, I'll abstain from going into in-depth lessons for the uninitiated. That all said, I have provided a glossary of TTRPG terms at the back of this book if you run across something you need a quick definition for.

Ready to get started? Great! Let's go.

PART I
WHY WE PLAY

CHAPTER 1

WHY DO WE FEEL SO HEROIC WHILE PLAYING *DUNGEONS & DRAGONS?*

A friend of mine once made an off-hand comment to our Friday night *Dungeons & Dragons* group that has stuck with me for years. "This is the highlight of my week," she said at the top of one session. "I start looking forward to playing this game by Monday morning." Things are better these days, but she didn't have much going on at the time she made that small confession. She was working as a ticket seller at a local botanical garden, which was in a pretty environment but didn't offer much in the way of new skill development or creative freedom. On top of that, she is normally cheerful and talkative, but selling tickets from behind a little window didn't give her a chance to have many meaningful interactions with people. I think a lot of us can identify with her on this. A lot of us have been there.

But on Friday nights, my friend got to play *Dungeons & Dragons*. All week she looked forward to doing all kinds of cool, meaningful heroics as Snickers, the goliath barbarian. She told me she loved controlling a character that got to be powerful and badass. She had, for example, a wide list of choices about how to play the game and how to role-play her character. We were all there with her, commenting on what she was doing, helping her learn the game as a first-time player, and cheering or laughing when she did something awesome. And *that* was why she looked forward to it. We all did and still do; this Friday night group has been going for over eight years as I write this.

This account of what draws someone to *Dungeons & Dragons* is only one of many I've heard about. I asked on social media for people to share why they enjoy playing the game and people flooded me with responses, most of which fit snugly into the same few themes. For example, a lot of people liked feeling heroic, powerful, and able to conquer the obstacles put before them. "It's because I have no real control over my life or the world," one Twitter user told me.[1] "I can make the story good, I can make it worth it, it can have a payoff." Others told me they loved the balance between playing by the rules and making meaningful choices about what kind of character to play and how to play them. One player noted, "It provides a lot more freedom than any video game, plus you're telling your party's story in a way unique to tabletop role-playing games." And, of course, people often said they enjoy *Dungeons & Dragons* because it lets them socialize, connect with people, and make new friends. "The living world created by our table felt like I had a real impact on it," wrote one player. "It also forces me to stop work and mindfully have fun with friends at least once a week."

I loved hearing these stories, but honestly it didn't surprise me, given what I've read about the psychology of motivation to engage in play and other voluntary activities. It sounds like a line of research centering around what's called **"Self Determination Theory"** (SDT). [2] In brief, the theory says we are motivated to engage in a voluntary activity to the extent that doing so lets us experience three things:

- **Competence**: getting better at something and improving our skills
- **Autonomy**: being able to exercise meaningful choices
- **Relatedness**: mattering to other people and having them recognize our efforts and accomplishments

Think of these as three psychological itches that feel good to scratch. If an activity soothes these itches, our engagement with it will be internally motivated; we'll do it for the sake of doing it.

Tabletop role-playing games like *Dungeons & Dragons* satisfy all three of these needs amazingly well. That goes a long way towards describing their timeless appeal and why so many of us choose to gather together, tell stories, level up our characters, and generate random numbers, despite having so many other ways to spend our time. In this chapter and the two that follow, I'll build a case for defining the "enjoyment" of *Dungeons & Dragons* as the satisfaction of our basic psychological needs for competence, autonomy, and relatedness. And you'll see how you can approach the hobby in ways that let you and others at the table enjoy it more. We'll even see how SDT has driven changes to the game's systems and how people play it. Let's begin with our need for competence.

COMPETENCE

Toddlers would be great at *Dungeons & Dragons* if the dice weren't a choking hazard. Just go loom over any nearby three-year-old and stare at them for a while. You'll see how natural it is for them to seek out new challenges and new skills to master through play. They explore the rules that govern their world, then try to find out how to push their own burgeoning capabilities like walking, talking, or simple puzzle-solving until they get it right and move on to a new challenge. This is SDT's definition of the need to experience competence: the satisfaction gotten by rising to challenges and getting better at something. Opportunities to acquire new capabilities, being challenged at a level that pushes us to improve, and getting feedback about our successes all satisfy this need.[3]

In the world of sports, this could mean pursuing and achieving new personal records for distance ran, weight lifted, or games won in a season. In the world of work, the need for competence could be satisfied by learning a new skill and successfully applying it. In video games, it could mean climbing up the leaderboard ranks or checking off a list of achievements. In the context of tabletop role-playing games (TTRPGs), it relates to both the mechanics of the game and to the content of your adventures. Leveling up your character and unlocking new play options creates a spike of perceived competence, as does learning to play a class effectively or even defeating a tough combat challenge. Similarly, good game masters fill players' time with progressively more and more difficult challenges and objectives for them to reach. Sure, you started off protecting a caravan from bandits, but that was level one. Who would be motivated to keep playing a game where you stay level one fighting bandits forever? Eventually, you want to protect the town, then the kingdom, then the world, and by level 20 you want to save entire planes of existence. (Or maybe destroy them – I'm not here to judge you.) The point is, this is why we all love to hear "Time to level up!" Those words signify progression, mastery, and new challenges, which make the game fun to play for its own sake. And, of course, the opposite of leveling up is incredibly demotivating, as the designers of *Dungeons & Dragons* have begrudgingly grown to admit over the years.

 ## LEVEL DRAIN AND MOTIVATIONAL DRAIN

Geoffrey Englestein is an award-winning author and tabletop game creator who teaches game design at New York University. A while back, he came on my podcast to talk about the psychology of game design and his newly published book about how losing things, including a sense of mastery or progression, demotivates players.[4] One idea that struck me was how not wanting to take things away from players has shaped the evolution of *Dungeons & Dragons* from edition to edition, starting with *Advanced Dungeons & Dragons* in the 1970s up to today's most recent edition.

This means it has become harder to frighten players in later editions of *Dungeons & Dragons*. Characters in the fourth and fifth editions are heartier and more powerful than in previous versions, and there's a greater focus on stories and characters. Game masters often don't want to undermine that with player death or other major setbacks. Your characters are heroic, and "heroes are fundamentally masterful in their ability to overcome challenges and grow in strength and ability," according to SDT researchers Scott Rigby and Richard Ryan.[5]

But this wasn't always the case. Character death was more common in previous editions and once upon a time the game even included something much worse: level drain. I dug out my original *Advanced Dungeons & Dragons Monster Manual* from 1977 and looked at the entry for "Wight," a nasty undead creature.[6] The second paragraph contains this horrifying gem:

> Because these monsters exist simultaneously on the normal and negative planes of the material plane, they are affected only by silver or magical weapons. This existence allows them to drain life energy levels —one such level each time they score a hit on an opponent. The creature so hit loses the hit points of damage scored (1-4) plus one experience level and all the bonuses derived from that level, i.e. hit dice, class bonuses, thief abilities, spell levels, etc. A 9th level magic user struck by a wight loses 1-4 hit points and he becomes an 8th level magic user...[7]

Yeah. That's right. If a wight hit your character, *you lost a level*. And it felt terrible because your psychological need for mastery took a hit when you lost those stats, spells, and abilities. In his book, *Achievement Relocked: Loss Aversion and Game Design* Englestein writes:

> In later versions, D&D third edition and version "3.5," level drain was modified by allowing players to make a saving roll to prevent a level loss. But if the roll failed, the level was permanently lost. In fourth and subsequent editions, level drain was completely removed. The undead creatures that used to have it now put effects on characters like weaken or immobilize –which could be cured through normal means within the game.[8]

You see this approach in game design all the time, where permanent character losses are avoided for the sake of enjoyment and to satisfy our need for mastery. Dying in a video game so that you have to restart a level or take a hit to your score is one thing, and it's usually presented as feedback, so it can be motivational if the player can eventually succeed. But permanent death or level drain in a story-driven TTRPG is far more severe and should be rare if the goal is to keep everyone at the table engaged.

The same concept holds on a smaller scale for temporary debuffs that reduce a player's perceived competence, like taking a penalty to dice rolls on account of being poisoned, immobilized, charmed, or blinded. It doesn't have to, though. As a game master, you can reframe such hits to competence to make them seem less like losses. For example, say a player character flagrantly disregards the "Do Not Disturb" sign on an ancient sarcophagus and is cursed by an annoyed mummy, so that she takes a minus-two penalty to her defense for the following 24 hours. Sure, the incautious player is at fault, but she would still be mildly annoyed and demotivated by the loss of competence. The game master, armed with the knowledge of self-determination theory but still wanting to punish a reckless player, could instead have the curse grant all enemies a plus-two bonus to their attacks against the afflicted character. Mathematically it's the same, but psychologically it feels better.

ROCKS FALL, EVERYONE DIES: GAME MASTER VS. PLAYERS

Though it had been used in the TTRPG community previously, the phrase "rocks fall, everyone dies" was made more widely famous by a 2002 installment of the Something Positive webcomic.[9] In the comic, a frustrated game master deals with an annoying player by exerting her control over in-game reality so that "rocks fall, everyone dies." No saving throw, no casting "Protection From Boulder," no way around it. You annoyed the game master; face the consequences.

It's a good joke, but "game master versus players" is a bad way to run a game because of what we know about the need for mastery. For example, I've seen game masters try to counter player abilities by contriving a way to stifle the player's competence. For example, say a player's wizard can cast the "Banishment" spell to shove a powerful enemy over to another plane of existence for a while. The party can then quickly clear the room of minions and ready actions to annihilate the banished enemy when they return from their brief interplanar vacation. A game master who would rather the fight go according to *his* script could arbitrarily make the monster immune to banishment. Too bad, so sad, Mr. Wizard. Or let's say another player's rogue specializes in poison and has worked to acquire the skills and equipment needed to coat every blade, arrow, and harsh word with deadly ichor. A game master who thinks this is too powerful could only put the party up against creatures that are immune to poison.

These seem like jerk moves, but I sympathize with the game masters in these situations. Sometimes you put a lot of work into an epic encounter or have a whole scenario mapped out in your head only to have someone circumvent it with a well-placed, 4th-level spell. Some power-gamers love finding strategies and synergies that trivialize anything the game master throws at them. That can be frustrating, but simply nullifying what the player has built their character to do is incredibly demotivating because subtracts from their sense of competence. You are making players less competent by taking abilities away from their characters—abilities that they worked for and see as demonstrations of their growth and achievement. It feels bad. The same is often true when game masters try to deplete characters' resources by making them go through many small-to-medium battles and traps to wick away all those high-level spell slots, potions, daily abilities, and other resources before the big, "real" battle. When the players finally get there, they're so wrung out and impotent that their chances of satisfying their need for competence are minute.

One resolution to this dilemma that I like is described by author and podcaster Mike "sly flourish" Shea in a blog post about what he calls "lightning rods."[10] Instead of trying to counter powerful character abilities, Shea recommends leaning into them by altering scenarios to allow players to change the tide of battles or otherwise set their characters up for success. One such lightning rod might be bottlenecking a horde of lower-level skeletons in a hallway so that the sorcerer can blast them all to bits with a line of lightning bolts—they're almost a literal lightning rod in this case. Or throw in a highly threatening brute of a creature that has to be dealt with immediately, but give it a low wisdom score, so it will likely fall prey to a polymorph spell or some other debilitating debuff.

Don't deny players the opportunity to do awesome stuff and feel competent. Instead, present them with the chance to do it but offer them challenges on other fronts in the same encounter or activity. As another *Dungeons & Dragons* content creator and Youtuber Ginny Di put it in a video about game mastering advice:

> This is sometimes called the "shoot your monks principle," referencing the monk class ability to deflect missiles. If you have the choice between never using ranged weapons against your monk or using ranged weapons and maybe adding a few more enemies or increasing the projectile damage to balance it …which one do you think the monk would have more fun playing? Both encounters can be equally challenging. The only difference is that in the latter example, the monk gets to do a really cool thing that only monks can do.[11]

The core message is that game masters shouldn't be afraid to create situations and encounters that lean into powerful character abilities, and neither should they make knee-jerk changes to the fabric of reality when players surprise them with their competence. It's demotivating and hurts player engagement because it tanks their sense of competence.

FAILING FORWARD AND SUCCEEDING AT A COST

Even with the most psychologically savvy game masters, failures will happen because games have rules. Without its rules, *Scrabble* isn't meaningfully different from typing. In TTRPGs, sometimes even a vulnerable enemy makes its saving throw and causes a player's cool spell to fizzle. Sometimes you roll poorly and your bard's speech is more insulting than persuasive, even though the palace guard was friendly to start with. It happens.

However, our need for mastery can still be soothed in the face of failure. One philosophy adopted by many game masters and players alike is known as "failing forward." The idea is that if players fumble into failure, something beneficial could still come out of it. It just takes a little imagination and description. If a sorcerer flings a firebolt at an enemy archer and misses, the flaming projectile could hit a tapestry behind the monster instead, setting it alight and forcing the foe to move out of cover on its turn. Flubbing an intimidation check on a drunk in the bar could earn the respect and assistance of another patron who admires the character's gusto. In each case, the player didn't get what they wanted, but they got something positive, albeit of lesser value.

Psychologist Mike Dixon and his colleagues call this **disguising losses as wins** and conducted a study to show how it can still be engaging.[12] The researchers hooked subjects up to machines to monitor their heart rates and skin conductivity, both measures of how excited someone is. Then they had subjects play "Lucky Larry's Lobstermania," a virtual slot machine game where players can bet on multiple "lines of play" meaning that they could make a winning combination out of symbols on any contiguous line drawn through the play field. For example, they could bet that taking the symbols from the top row first column, the middle row second column, and the bottom row third column could make a winning combination. And they could make as many of these bets as they wanted, so it was frequently the case that betting on many lines in one spin might result in a small win. But since betting on each line cost money, the math was such that it netted a loss—a loss disguised as a win, given that the game would still celebrate the matchup of three winning symbols on a single play line. Subjects in the study got excited when they lost but it was disguised as winning. They weren't as excited as when they got more money back than they put in, but they were happier than they were when they experienced a complete loss.

This effect of losses disguised as wins maps cleanly onto the "failing forward concept," especially with TTRPG systems designed to evoke it. One of the mechanics from the *Star Wars Roleplaying Game* has an unusual dice system that does this. It lets the dice focus on storytelling instead of binary success/fail outcomes for an attempted task. Using this system, players roll up to six types of dice when they want to do something like pilot an X-wing through a debris field or blast an oncoming stormtrooper. Three of the dice are "positive" and relate to how good the character is at the attempted task and how advantageous circumstances are for them. The other dice are "negative" and relate to how difficult the task is and what forces are working against them. Some results from the "positive" dice cancel out results from the "negative" dice and vice versa.

Here's a quick example: a player shoots at a group of stormtroopers rushing through a blast door. The story dice turn up no "successes"—the shot goes wide—but they do net an "advantage" result. So the missed shot hits the blast door controls, causing them to partially close and inconvenience the last few stormtroopers still beyond the doorway. Not as big a win as eliminating an enemy, but still a bit satisfying and exciting on balance. The system has disguised a loss as a win and the player has failed forward. The same principles encountered by the experimental subjects gambling on Lucky Larry's Lobstermania come into play, though in a way that doesn't cost anyone anything. The idea is that in addition to unambiguously succeeding or failing in an action, results might occupy a space between the two. A player's need for competence isn't satisfied as thoroughly as if they had fully succeeded, without any downsides, but that itch is scratched enough to keep them motivated until the next opportunity to do something awesome comes around.

Based on everything above, we can see how *Dungeons & Dragons* players are often motivated to play the game because of the sense of competence it provides and because of the chance at mastering the complex challenges that comes with it. But other aspects of the design and structure of TTRPGs also make them motivating. For example, their imagination-driven, freeform nature gives you more freedom than any other kind of game. In the next chapter, we will explore the second of Self-Determination Theory's motivators: autonomy.

WHAT YOU LEARNED IN THIS CHAPTER

- Competence, sometimes called mastery, is the first of the psychological needs from Self-Determination Theory.
- We are motivated to do something to the extent that doing so will give us a sense of competence, or being able to successfully do something, grow in ability, and take on tougher challenges.
- In TTRPGs, competence can be satisfied both through the mechanics of the game and through the narrative of your character's actions.
- People hate to have this sense of power and mastery taken away from them, as evidenced by the abandonment of permanent death and level-drain over the course of *Dungeons & Dragons's* development.

HOW TO APPLY THIS CHAPTER TO YOUR GAME

- If you're a game master, don't stifle players' chances to feel competent by taking things away from them or hard-countering their abilities; put obstacles in their path that let them use their cool abilities and knowledge *in addition* to challenging them.
- Game masters should let players "fail forward" by making something good happen even when they roll poorly—just not as good as if they had rolled well—and players should learn to argue for such outcomes.

- As a player, don't be afraid to describe your character's actions in terms that paint them as competent.
- As a game master, do the same for your players whenever you can.

CHAPTER 2

WHY IS THE OPEN-ENDED FREEDOM OF DUNGEONS & DRAGONS SO APPEALING?

While in college, I worked at a toy store in the mall. It paid terribly but it was a ton of fun because I got to indulge my inner child by checking out an entire store's worth of toys and talking with customers about which Ninja Turtle they should buy for their little cousin's birthday (it depended on the kid's personality, but I almost always recommended Raphael). One of my favorite parts of the job was coming in to open the store and build the displays. We were supposed to populate them with interactive toys like robotic dogs, electronic games, and dress-up items that would get people's attention and pull foot traffic into the store. However, we were also supposed to include things that companies had paid us to promote. These instructions came to us via memos from our corporate office each week and they were very specific. But I didn't like to do exactly as I was told. I liked to build out my own displays. I'd make an eclectic tea party where transforming robots socialized with Teddy Ruxpin and My Little Pony characters or a summer-themed display where mechanical, dancing flowers showcased different outdoor games and baseball trading cards. The store manager had other things to worry about, so this became a way for me to have fun whenever I worked the opening shift. That is, until I got slapped down for it by our district manager.

Let's call him Kevin because his name was Kevin. He was new to the job and had well-defined ideas about merchandising.

He visited my store one Saturday morning when I had set up a display in direct violation of the corporate-mandated promotional plan. I think Darth Vader and Stretch Armstrong were playing a game of *Hungry Hungry Hippos*. He took one look at the display and began berating the manager, citing the store memo, and demanding that we set up displays "the right way." I could only stand to the side, looking chagrinned and apologetic. Kevin then proceeded to find other sins among the store shelves, including incorrect displays on end cabinets, a misplaced rack of batteries, and the shocking presence of a foam mat that I had placed—out of customers' sight—behind the cash register to take some of the pressure off my feet and back when I stood for hours on end.

It's amazing how one man took something that should be inherently fun and engaging—working in a toy store—and turned it into something boring, mechanical, and rote. Kevin, if you're reading this, I hope you're happy.[1] Because I still think about your visit that day and I frequently use it as my go-to anecdote about the second psychological need described by self-determination theory: **autonomy.** This concept describes how we are motivated to engage in activities that allow us meaningful choices. Would you rather read only what others tell you to or would you like to create your own library, specific to your interests? Would you prefer a job where you have some flexibility to do your work as you see fit or would you rather perform rote actions all day according to the rigid instructions in a corporate memo?

For most of us, the answers to these questions are obvious, but not always realistic. We spend our time at work, school, or other parts of life with limited autonomy, limited choice about how we do our thing, and limited opportunity to make meaningful decisions. As one early game studies researcher succinctly noted, "A gamer, today's Everyman, is battered by forces outside his control;

he is at the mercy of restrictions, superiors, and bureaucrats."[2] Fortunately, this is where games like *Dungeons & Dragons* shine. When you sit down at the table our real-life responsibilities and constraints drop away. TTRPGs are specifically built to indulge our desire for meaningful choice, whether it's in tactical combat or in determining how the story at the table unfolds. You can't smite Barry from the budget office for denying your procurement request, but when you sit down at the table to play *Dungeons & Dragons* you have many fewer restraints. You have control. You can make the story what we want it to be. You can make decisions that feel right to you.

Volition, choice, and decisions energize us and keep us engaged in an activity. A long list of research shows that when we are allowed autonomy in school or work, we tend to stick with it and perform better.[3,4] But autonomy doesn't mean absolute freedom, anarchy, and spasms of freeform jazz. For a situation to satisfy our desire for autonomy, it needs to offer *meaningful* choices. It needs to be *you* finding an option that speaks to you and that aligns with your values and self-determined direction. This means that, ironically, we may feel the greatest sense of autonomy when we are constrained by our values, vision, or ethics. (Or those of our characters, as we'll explore in the chapter on the psychology of morality and alignment systems.)

In *Dungeons & Dragons,* you can create, customize, and develop your character with various builds, equipment, spells, feats, skills, and backgrounds. I'll cover the psychology behind how we deal with these sometimes overwhelming options in a later chapter, but let's recognize here that when the time comes for combat, exploration, or social interactions, players get to decide what happens. From picking which enemy to attack to deciding how to phrase their persuasive appeal to a noble who might support their cause, players are in charge. "A 9th-level spellcaster has more choices than a Cheesecake Factory menu," quips one *Dungeons & Dragons* YouTube creator who goes by the name "Professor Dungeon Master."[5]

Except, of course, when the game master decides to rip out a few pages from that menu and disallow certain choices.

BANNED AT THE TABLE: LIMITING PLAYER CHOICE

I once ran a short adventure for my child's friends where the party would be tasked with retrieving a lockbox from a derelict merchant ship overrun by undead monstrosities. One of the players rolled up an unconventional character that would be able to both fly and hold its breath indefinitely. Having planned out the nautical adventure and its hurdles, I knew that this combination would both trivialize key challenges and probably leave the rest of the players out of the fun. So I told the player that she couldn't play the character race she had chosen. The adventure then went more or less as I had planned, but I could tell the player was annoyed and I felt chagrinned, thinking I should have handled that situation better. I probably lost a few points on my "Cool Dad" score, too.

I'm not alone, though. Not in the cool dad thing, but in terms of taking player options off the table to better suit my plans. Game masters frequently make calls to limit player choices for the sake of balancing encounters, maintaining a consistent tone, or making the game easier to run. And despite what I've said so far about the need for autonomy, these aren't always bad calls! Arguments can be made that certain combinations of character features are unbalanced and need to be curbed. I have a friend who thinks the

"Sharpshooter" feat in *Dungeons & Dragons* is too powerful since a level one character who takes it can put an arrow between the eyes of an enemy hiding behind cover 300 feet away, doing enough damage to murder it in one shot. So my friend prohibits players from choosing that feat. I know another game master who hates how "cuddly" *Dungeons & Dragons 5th Edition* has become, with all the animal-like races such as cat people, turtle people, bird people, rabbit people, horse people, a different kind of bird people, snake people, lizard people, and a *third* kind of bird people. So none of that, he says. Play a human, elf, or dwarf like God intended.

But even if these house rules and lists of banned choices are justified based on fairness and facilitating a story the group wants to tell, they can still be demotivating and cause disengagement. On top of that, we hate to have choices taken away from us once we feel like we have them—even if we didn't intend to take them. This is a well-understood effect called **psychological reactance**, coined back in the 1960s by psychologist Jack Brehm.[6],[7] Most parents are probably familiar with the concept if they've ever seen one of their kids jealously guard a previously ignored toy as soon as their sibling expresses interest in playing with it. It happens in adults, too. One study on the subject followed the shopping habits of homemakers from Florida who learned that a certain type of laundry soap was going to be discontinued in their state because of environmentally harmful ingredients. Once they knew they were going to be unable to possess the sudsy good, shoppers formed caravans to travel to neighboring states and stock up.[8] It was the same attitude as with the children's toys or "going out of business" sales: People don't want it until they think they won't be able to have it.

With *Dungeons & Dragons* and other TTRPGs, the key is to discuss taking choices off the table as early as possible and give everyone a say in the house rules. The game master shouldn't try to clip autonomy's wings after a player has chosen a specific character option or declared an action. The better time is during what's often called "session zero," where everyone gets together at the start of a new campaign to lay down the ground rules. What kind of story will this be? What topics, situations, and acts should be taboo and absent from the campaign (e.g., sexual violence or animal cruelty)? What spells, feats, or subclasses should be omitted and *why* should they be omitted? For the sake of game balance? Making the game easier to run? Because the game master doesn't own that rulebook? And we all agree that we're playing tortle monks named after Renaissance painters, right?

The key is that everyone should be part of the discussion about these house rules and lists of banned options. If they are, they are less likely to see the choices as available in the first place and thus be less likely to feel psychological reactance. Also, session zero discussions give players a head start on dreaming up characters that act and think in ways that, while limiting their role-playing and tactical options, still allow them to make *meaningful* choices within the constraints they've built for the character. Which will still be motivating.

Of course, the beginning of a campaign isn't the only place where autonomy can be lost. Sometimes it happens at every point from start to end, like a train on a track.

RAILROADING PLAYERS

Years ago, I was a player in a game where the party was attempting to storm a castle so we could steal critical intelligence and assassinate a bothersome hobgoblin general. The game master had prepared a gauntlet of fights and environmental hazards that led through the front gates, into a well-defended courtyard, down several trapped hallways, past housewares, and into the enemy general's private sanctum at the back of the stronghold.

"Okay," I said. "Let's approach from the south and I'll cast Passwall to create a five-foot-wide tunnel through the back wall of the castle. Much easier."

The game master, panicking, flipped through his rulebook to look up the description for the Passwall spell. "Ummm," he said, "this says the passage can be up to 20 feet deep."

"Yes?" I asked, not liking where this was going.

"The walls of this castle are 25 feet deep."

I let that hang in the air for a moment. "Twenty-five-foot thick *walls*?"

"Yes. They built this place sturdy. Front gate, then?"

With apologies to the game master, who is still a friend and part of my gaming group, this was an example of nullifying the cool power a player could use as I described in the previous chapter on Competence. It was also a double-whammy because it was simultaneously an example of "railroading" players. This happens when game masters take away player agency and curtail choices so that any action inevitably leads to a predetermined scene, story beat, or outcome. It's like cruising through the adventure on railroad tracks instead of going off-road.

And once again, we may find ourselves sympathizing with game masters even as they lay down these linear rails. Maybe they put in a lot of prep time. Maybe they're trying to do what they think will be most fun for us. Maybe the players are being insufferably creative and unpredictable. Yet taking agency away from players saps the game's ability to satisfy our need for autonomy and results in less motivation to play.

But it doesn't have to be this way. The best game masters find ways to maintain linear campaigns and plots while giving the players agency and even a feeling of autonomy where there isn't any. One technique is what the tabletop role-playing community has taken to calling "Schrodinger's dungeon" or sometimes "Schrodinger's railroad." These terms reference the famous thought experiment dreamed up by Erwin Schrodinger to illustrate how something (like a cat) can have its fate linked to quantum mechanics such that it simultaneously exists in multiple states (like dead and alive). Until, that is, someone observes it directly at which point it settles down and stops violating our cherished assumptions about reality. Extending this idea to creating the illusion of autonomy in *Dungeons & Dragons* could mean that an ogre the game master wants the party to fight is simultaneously behind the door on the left *and* the door on the right. One ogre is simultaneously in both places until someone opens one of the doors. Then the ogre is only behind that one and was never behind the other. Players still get to decide where to go, but the game master can move encounters, non-player characters, and even entire locations around behind the scenes. Did the players miss an important item that they needed? Now it's in the next place they're headed, and it always has been. Such are the game master's reality-bending powers. This approach has its limits, of course. If the players decide to visit a mountain aerie and instead find themselves in an underwater temple that the game master had hoped they would visit, the players are going to catch on. But it works surprisingly well when used subtly.

Another approach to avoid railroading while still allowing the game master to prepare is to adopt a linear plot at a sufficiently high level that allows for player agency. Say that your party needs to escape from a prison, recruit an ally to help them go underground, find evidence to clear their names, and confront the bad guy that set them up. That's a pretty high-level outline for an adventure that leaves the players with lots of autonomy. How will they escape prison? Will they go searching for someone to hide them or will they rely on one of the several contacts they've established in town? What evidence can they think of that would clear their name and how would they acquire it? Do they confront the bad guy by swinging swords or by staging a dramatic and damning reveal in front of the duke? Those are still a lot of choices! Now compare that linear, yet high-level, adventure with the highly mapped out plan: "You must escape the prison by picking the lock and fighting the guards. Then you must roll a successful Persuasion check on the innkeeper you met last session to convince him to hide you. Then you have to sneak into the enemy's mansion and take back the magic crown he stole from the duke. Then you have to present it to the duke to prove your innocence." Which session would give you more autonomy and which one sounds like it was written by a certain district manager of a toy store?[9]

MAKE YOUR OWN AUTONOMY

When I was a kid, the highlight of every month was the day a new issue of *Dragon* magazine came out. The magazine was distributed by TSR, the publisher of *Dungeons & Dragons* at the time, and it included all kinds of amazing art, supplementary rules, and product reviews. My favorite issues were the April Fool's editions that contained joke material that often tickled my weird sense of humor. One feature in an April 1985 issue always stuck in my mind. It was called "Nogard: The High-Level Adventure to End All Adventures."[10] The art accompanying the piece features a max-level character bristling with confidence and items of legendary power, standing on a featureless gray plane with nothing else on it. The entire joke of the so-called adventure (besides being "Dragon" spelled backward) is that the only way to defeat such a high-level hero is to present them with nothing to do until the player gets bored, gives up, and writes "RETIRED" across the top of the character sheet. I think about that now 30-year-old joke article more often than I'd like. Not because I retire many high-level characters, but because I sometimes feel like I'm playing in that gaping, featureless plane straight out of Nogard where I have no meaningful or interesting choices to make every time my turn comes around. Fortunately, it's avoidable if you're on the lookout for it.

One of my biggest pet peeves as a *Dungeons & Dragons* player is when fighting breaks out in a plain, featureless room or stretch of wilderness, where combat is played out on a blank battle map or a theater in a mind that seems to be suffering from a concussion. Tactical options, environmental effects, and role-playing are ignored in favor of not-so-thrilling narration like "The ogre walks over and hits you for 15 damage." This is opposed to encounters with features built into them that make things interesting and offer opportunities for new tactical choices or scene-specific role-playing. Give me terrain that grants me cover or access to different levels of elevation. Give me environmental effects like wind, thin ice, burning buildings, quicksand, rockslides, panicking crowds, or dilapidated bridges that I must work around to my advantage or entertainment. Give me ticking time bombs (literal or metaphorical) like nearly completed summoning rituals or rising flood waters. Let me decide between dealing with what's in front of my character right now or going after the archer perched on a ledge and shooting at me from above.

Things like this aren't just possible in *Dungeons & Dragons*, the game practically begs for game masters to introduce them. Having these choices creates a sense of autonomy; the game is designed to have players interact with the environment and other characters, especially during the combat and exploration parts. Rogues can choose to hide behind cover to activate their sneak attack class feature. Fighters high in the Athletics skill can try to shove enemies off ledges. Wizards can use a spell to enlarge an elevator's counterweight so that it can't be used by monsters in pursuit of the party. The possibilities are endless and require only a bit of creativity by game masters to set up scenarios that spike players' sense of autonomy.

That said, game masters aren't the only ones responsible for avoiding the grey, featureless plane of Nogard. Players need to speak up and ask about the environment so they can propose cool things to do in it. If you as a player come into a bandit lair, you should ask questions like "Is there a chandelier hanging from the ceiling?" or "Is there a fire brazier nearby?" or even "Are there a bunch of crates piled precariously on the ledge above the leader?" Give your game master ideas. Then propose that you swing from the chandelier to clobber the spellcaster in the back, kick the brazier of burning coals into the bandit captain's face, or sneak around and topple the heavy crates onto the enemies below. You don't have to just swing your sword and do 1d8 damage. You have choices! But sometimes we don't think of them because we look at the battle map or listen to the description of an environment and assume that it's complete and immutable, that there's nothing for your rogue to hide behind or nothing to set on fire because you don't see it or hear it mentioned. You must remember to lobby for those meaningful choices and hope the game master understands the importance of satisfying your need for autonomy for the health of the game.

WHAT YOU LEARNED IN THIS CHAPTER

- Self-determination theory holds that we will be motivated to engage in an activity to the extent that it provides us with meaningful choices that fit within our goals, character, and values.
- Psychological reactance is the phenomenon where we place much more value on having a choice once we think it's going to be taken away.
- Our need for autonomy at least partially explains why "save or die" situations can be so demotivating.

HOW TO APPLY THIS CHAPTER TO YOUR GAME

- Only take away options and choices if you have an understandable, productive reason for doing so.
- If you think you have that good a reason, negotiate those changes in a "session zero" at the beginning of the campaign so it doesn't feel like they're being taken away in the moment.
- This is also a good time to discuss *behaviors* that players and the game masters should not engage in, either as characters or as players.
- Railroading players and limiting their choices is demotivating and the game master can often create a better effect with plot points at a sufficiently high level to allow players plenty of choice as to how they move between them.

- As a game master, create rich environments for combat and exploration, the kinds that offer players creative, satisfying choices that play into their characters' skills and idioms.
- As a player, ask questions about the environment until you get an answer that gives you fun and interesting choices.

CHAPTER 3
WHY DO WE LOVE FEELING IMPORTANT TO BOTH REAL AND IMAGINARY PEOPLE?

Back in early 2009, I was lonely. I had a wife and two young kids who were (and still are) great points of light in my life, but I also craved meaningful interactions with others outside of my family. Especially other adults. I had just moved to another city and all of my old friends from college and graduate school were scattered. Neither was I making any friends at work, where my interactions with co-workers felt transactional and nobody cared about the weird stuff I was into. Honestly, 90% of my job was sending emails to people so they could do work that didn't affect me. It was some serious ennui.

In search of a solution, I got on meetup.com, which is a website that connects people based on their interests—be they photography, bar hopping, political movements, or tabletop role-playing games. I had heard that the new, 4th edition of *Dungeons & Dragons* ("4E") had come out and I was interested in getting back into the hobby after a decades-long break. I put myself out there, explained who I was, let people know what I was looking for, and started some conversations. Not long after, I got an email from a guy named Andrew who said, "Hey we posted back and forth on the message board, and I think we should be able to work with Fridays. Don't worry we aren't crazy psychos or rules lawyers or anything. If you don't know 4E don't worry we are all still learning as well." That email kicked off my access to a source of social interaction and enjoyment that continues to this day. People have come and gone from that group, but I'm still playing *Dungeons & Dragons* with some of them every Friday night, 15 years later.

In the previous chapters, I discussed how the design and experience of tabletop role-playing games satisfy Self-Determination Theory's psychological needs for competence and autonomy. And while feeling heroic and making meaningful choices are the main ingredients in my enjoyment of *Dungeons & Dragons*, what I look forward to every session more than anything is spending time with friends and engaging in a communal exercise where the choices I make enhance others' enjoyment of the game. Even more so if I'm the game master for that session. Tabletop role-playing games are designed to connect us to other people. You can show up to a new group or sit down at a table at a gaming convention and immediately start talking about the game without making painful small talk about the weather or trying to make what you do for a living sound more interesting than it is. The game is designed to be cooperative and social in that it constantly requires players to overcome challenges *together*. The game is its own icebreaker.

I'm not alone in my appreciation for the social aspects of tabletop role-playing games. In one survey of role-playing gamers by researchers at the University of Helsinki, 70% of respondents agreed that role-playing friends made up a significant percentage of their social circle.[1] Eighty-seven percent said they had formed significant friendships or other relationships through the hobby. Not only that, but these gaming relationships often acted as springboards to broader friendships, with 100% of the survey respondents saying that they met up with their fellow players for activities outside of the game.

Games like *Dungeons & Dragons* facilitate meaningful social interactions so well because it's nice for someone to tell us how relevant we are to them. When we feel that someone recognizes our impact on them and their lives, this satisfies the third psychological need according to Self-Determination Theory: **relatedness**. While the importance of belonging to a group for our mental well-being is well established,[2] the value of scratching this psychological itch through gaming has also been shown. One group of researchers studied multiplayer online games, a genre that marries aspects of TTRPGs and video games. The researchers found that, relative to other kinds of games, the opportunities for interactions with other players made these games especially effective at satisfying the need for relatedness, which itself is correlated with enjoyment.[3] One other study found the same effect on a smaller scale when they looked at the video game *Wii Sports Bowling* and compared those who played it single-player with those who played with a cooperative partner. Merely playing with another person led to greater perceptions of relatedness and fun.

I expect the same to be true of games like *Dungeons & Dragons* where everything we do at the table affects what experiences other players and the game master have. When I surveyed people online about what motivated them to play TTRPGs, most of them mentioned something about the chance to engage in social interactions, whether they be with old friends or strangers in a drop-in game at a hobby shop. "This is one of the things that keeps me coming back," wrote one player named David. "If it wasn't for *Dungeons & Dragons* there are important people in my life who might not still be in my social circle. It keeps us connected and there's more at stake than just showing up for a poker night or a dinner date."

HOW TO RELATE TO OTHER PLAYERS

In their book, *Glued to Games*, researchers Scott Rigby and Richard Ryan note that three things create a sense of relatedness in these kinds of interactions: **acknowledgment, support, and impact**.[4] Let's look at each in turn.

If you want your fellow players to have a good time, one simple thing you can do is **acknowledge** what they're doing. According to Rigby and Ryan, acknowledgment happens when we feel that we have someone's full attention. Any game master that sees players looking at their cell phones or idly stacking dice is missing the acknowledgment that will make them feel related. Conversely, players who lean forward, take notes, cheer on other players, and toss out the occasional "good job!" are acknowledging other players and the game master, which will motivate them to stay engaged. One of the kindest things a player can do for a game master at the end of the night is to say, "Thanks for running, I had a great time." Some game masters will tear up upon hearing this. I've seen it. This is particularly important in online games where it's hard to gauge other people's level of engagement. In past games, I've taken on the role of party historian and note-taker, creating online repositories of lore and NPC profiles that showed the game master that I appreciated their work enough and found it interesting.

Next, while telling someone, "Good job!" is nice, we also want others to provide **emotional and mental support** for what we're doing. We want them to understand us and want us to have a good time. Players who are there to hog the spotlight, dominate the party debates, and litigate rules aren't there to support other players in their quest to satisfy all their psychological needs. Game masters who are unwilling to adapt their game to match the tone, content, or heroic storytelling that players want are not engaging in emotional and mental support. We experience relatedness when those around us actively support us in our efforts to satisfy Self-Determination Theory's other needs of competence and autonomy. Fortunately, the way many tabletop role-playing games are designed encourages this by emphasizing roles, skills, and imaginative play. Healers like clerics or paladins support other players by keeping them upright and alive. Melee combatants and wizards control the battlefield and support those looking for an opportunity to land a sneak attack or a well-placed spell. If you've ever pulled off a one-two combo of the Entangle and Stinking Cloud spells then you know what I mean. The interconnectedness of the game design allows us to support each other and feel critically related.

Finally, we matter to other people when we have an **impact** on them. If we do things that benefit or even harm others, we feel a sense of relatedness to that person (or dragon). Did you heal your fellow player's character to bring her back from the brink of death? Impact. Rescued the blacksmith's apprentice from the clutches of an ogre? Impact. Foiled the greedy vizir's schemes? Impact. What this means is that every time you cooperate with another player, change the state of the game world, or perform another act of heroism, you're having an impact on someone—even if they're not sitting at the table with you—and satisfying your need for relatedness to some degree.

MATTERING TO NPCS

Some researchers studying video games have suggested that our need for relatedness is also satisfied by interacting with non-player characters controlled by computer code. And why not? NPCs can easily offer praise to acknowledge when we perform certain actions, and completing quests for them and earning their favor is the whole point of some games. Of the levers used to move relatedness described above, only support is hard for NPCs to pull off since we know that computer programs can't genuinely understand us and want us to have a good time.[5]

But in TTRPGs, NPCs can satisfy our need for relatedness much more effectively because they're controlled by a game master—a human being, often one with a penchant for backstories, funny voices, and general theatrics. Game masters can rewrite NPCs' stories on the fly in response to the players' actions. They can offer in-character praise of an intensity that human players might not provide for fear of making things weird. NPCs can describe the difference the player characters have made in their lives, be it for better or worse. And while everyone understands the line between make-believe and reality and thus knows that non-player characters aren't expressing *actual* care for players and their well-being, they probably realize when the game master is using an NPC as a proxy.

In practical terms, this means that if you're a player, you should interact with non-player characters instead of seeing them as vending machines for quests. You should pretend to talk to *them* instead of talking to the game master. Pay attention to and take notes on NPCs' backstories and their situations. See how they interconnect to the bigger story being told at the table. Think about how you're impacting the people and places around you, even if they only exist in the real world as stat blocks and maps. You'll find more opportunities to satisfy the need for relatedness if you do.

Similarly, if you're a game master, don't treat NPCs as window dressing. Roll with it when a player character interacts with an NPC and see what develops. Have them react when the players are talking about them as if they weren't there, as we often do. Keep a stash of names and simple personality traits that you can throw together in the moment, or pattern the NPC after a character in a work of existing fiction with a few twists to obscure your original source. Have NPCs curse the players or praise them for their actions, depending on the situation—either works as long as it communicates that the players are having an impact on that fictitious person. Additionally, make the players' actions matter to the world. Have NPCs die, prosper, or otherwise change *directly* as a result of what the player characters do. It'll go a long way toward making them feel important to someone else.

HOW PLAYERS CAN RELATE TO DUNGEON MASTERS

Earlier in this chapter, I explained how players can feel relatedness through acknowledgment, support, and information about their impact. People are often motivated to play TTRPGs because they are designed to satisfy the need for relatedness in these ways, both because of how their in-game characters matter to other characters (and non-player characters) and because of how the out-of-game players matter to one another. But there's often one person who gets left out because they're not playing a character in the same way: the game master. Sure, NPCs could sing the praises of the game master and throw them parades, but that's weird because players know that the NPCs are scripted by the game master. It's a little sad, I'm told. Instead, players are responsible for acknowledging the game master and letting them know the impact they're having on the game. Said one game master I spoke to online, "I work really hard all week to make something for three specific people to enjoy and usually they do! That feels good."

Not only that, but game masters often need feedback. Even if they're executing exactly the kind of game they intend to, that game may not fit with everyone else's expectations or desires. For example, running *Dungeons & Dragons* as a tactical combat simulator with an unalloyed threat of character death is a common way to play the game, but it's not a good fit if the players all want more role-playing, exploration, and story. Or players might not be interested in building out a home base of operations in a metropolis and may instead want to roam the countryside in search of adventure.

So who's going to talk to the game master? That conversation can be awkward to approach, and most players don't want to come across as an unappreciative malcontent. The good news is that psychologists have thoroughly studied how to give employees feedback about their job performance in ways that make them more likely to improve their performance. It's an imperfect analogy for game masters, since they aren't players' employees and game mastering usually isn't a job. However, the literature on feedback still has some good advice on how to make game masters feel acknowledged, impactful, and supported.

The first tip is to **give specific feedback**. Squishy, nonspecific feedback is less valuable and less likely to get the game master's attention. Don't tell them, "You could do better" or "I'm not having much fun" even if it's true. Instead, be more specific. Here are some examples of good and bad feedback:

Bad	Good
"Combat is boring"	"It would make things more fun if you incorporated the environment more in combat so we could have more tactical and creative options."
"I'm bored."	"I went two hours last session without rolling a single die or having my character do anything."
"Things move too slowly."	"You're letting the party spin its wheels too much instead of forcing us to make a decision and move on."
"You're too much of a stickler for the rules."	"We should embrace the 'rule of cool' and bend the other rules if it means we'll all laugh and talk about it later."

This approach is better because game masters probably want to know exactly what they're doing that isn't landing well so they can tweak it. Again, that doesn't necessarily mean that the game master doesn't know the rules or is incompetent. It could just mean that what they're doing would be fine at other tables, but not this group. After all, game masters have the same goals as players: have a good time and make fun stories.

A second tip is to **focus on behaviors, not the person**. People tend to discount or ignore feedback if it endangers their self-image. No game master wants to hear feedback that sounds like an attack on them as a person. It's far easier to convince them to change their behavior than it is to alter their self-perception and idea of who they are as a person. If you're giving feedback, focus on what the game master is doing and avoid language that sounds like you're picking on who they are.

Bad	Good
"You don't know the rules."	"You abruptly shut me down when I tried to clarify the rules for flanking."
"You seem like one of those game masters that want to kill the players."	"You didn't seem to balance that last combat encounter very fairly."
"You're not much of an actor, are you?"	"It would help us keep track of key NPCs if you described their mannerisms and voices a bit better."

Next, make sure to **give feedback quickly and frequently**. One of my friends used to not only ask for feedback about his skills as a game master, but he would do it after almost every session. Before he went to bed that night, he'd email a quick survey to all his players with questions like "What did you not like?" and

"What do you want more of?" This was great because research has shown that the more quickly feedback comes, the more likely we are to tie it to our performance and act on it.[6]

If your game master doesn't send out quick little surveys like this, you can still deliver quick feedback in the form of a side conversation on your way out the door, a quick chat online if you're playing remotely, or even an email or text (though see below about in-person vs. asynchronous feedback). What you want to avoid is waiting until the end of the campaign to try and look back at everything all at once. You won't be able to remember helpful details or specific behaviors, and even if you can recall something the opportunity to act on your feedback will be long gone.

The next tip is to **help the game master see progress**. One of the earliest theories of performance feedback is known as the control theory of feedback.[7] It says that when someone sets a goal, they seek out feedback to determine if they are getting closer to it. If I'm trying to run a five-kilometer race in under 30 minutes, I'll track my pace and distance whenever I run. If I'm trying to paint a band of hobgoblin miniatures in time for Saturday's game, I'll keep count of how many I've painted, how good they look, and how much time I've got left. Or even if I'm after a vaguer goal like creating memorable characters for my game, it helps me see my progress if I observe players talking about them and interacting with them.

Given this, it helps if the game master has goals. And it helps even more if their players know what those goals are. This is an important agenda item for "session zero" of a campaign where the whole group discusses and agrees on expectations. You as a player can directly ask the game master, "What are your goals for the game? How are you wanting to flex and stretch your muscles as a game master?" If you don't cover this in session zero, no problem. You can ask them at any time. Then, when you offer your feedback, it can make it much more appealing to the game master if it's couched in terms of progress (or not) toward their goals.

Finally, **people like to receive positive feedback in front of others and negative or constructive feedback in private**. Don't give negative feedback in the moment and in front of other players. That's a great time for praise, but constructive feedback will be most readily received if the game master feels no need to defend their reputation or save face in front of others. That said, don't take the easy way out of sending an email or text message if you can help it. Research has shown that face-to-face feedback is better, if for no other reason than that it can allow for two-way communication and clarification.[8] A game master may not know what encounter a player is referring to in their feedback, for example, or they may not have the same idea about what "more engaging" means. This might make players uncomfortable, especially if your relationship with the person is new or not yet cemented into a comfortable friendship, but it's the most effective way to do it.

While all these tips for giving good feedback can help players help game masters improve, and create a sense of relatedness on both sides, the tips can also be adapted for players to give fellow players feedback or for the game master to help players. Give players specific, timely feedback, praise spontaneously them in front of others, present constructive feedback in private, and focus on behaviors. Communication is key to relatedness for everyone at the table.

WHAT YOU LEARNED IN THIS CHAPTER

- Relatedness, the third psychological need described by Self-Determination Theory, holds that we are intrinsically motivated to engage in an activity if it makes us feel important to other people.
- Relatedness is facilitated by interactions conveying acknowledgment, support, and impact.
- Acknowledgment is simply giving someone your attention and acknowledging their actions.
- Support is when someone shows that they want us to be engaged and motivated, especially if they try to satisfy our other psychological needs for competence and autonomy.
- Impact is when we have a meaningful effect on others through our actions or decisions, or when others react strongly to what we do.
- We are motivated to feel relatedness towards other people such as other players at the table, but fictional, non-player characters can also satisfy this need.

HOW TO APPLY THIS CHAPTER TO YOUR GAME

- Players, the game master, and even non-player characters can satisfy our need for relatedness by acknowledging player actions, supporting them in their goals of satisfying their psychological needs, and helping them understand the impact they're having on others.

- Game masters should treat non-player characters like they are real people in terms of how they interact with the characters by making them react to what they do, supporting their drive toward self-determination, and describing how player characters' actions affect them.
- Make a habit of submitting feedback to your game master.
- For best results, give the feedback promptly (e.g., in the moment if it's positive) and make sure you describe specific behaviors instead of characteristics of the person.
- Give negative information privately and in person if you can; sending it asynchronously robs the recipient of the ability to ask for clarifying information.

CHAPTER 4
HOW DOES *DUNGEONS & DRAGONS* PULL US INTO IMAGINARY WORLDS?

Imagine that you are a *Dungeons & Dragons* player listening to the following description of your approach to a supposedly haunted house:

> After a long trek up a disused, four-mile road littered with fallen branches, you come upon a manor overlooking the sea. The cold rain comes slashing down, driven by howling winds that seem to want to send you tumbling over the cliff to the rocks below. You all enter the tangle of the manor's front garden, now long overgrown with weeds and vines. This square area is roughly 80 feet to a side and is hemmed in by a black iron fence. You smell dank earth, rot, and stagnant water. There's a large, debris-choked fountain at the center of the garden and an overgrown hedge maze to the east. The main house is a squat, two-story structure that looms at the far north end of the garden, opposite the rusty gate you came through. Its roof has been ripped away in several places by coastal storms, but the only entrance on the ground floor looks to be the front door, which hangs open and crooked on its hinges. Those of you with a passive Perception of at least 15 think you see a light flicker in one of the upstairs windows, but you can't be sure it wasn't just lightning reflecting off the remains of the shattered glass. Okay. What do you want to do?

That description isn't too far from one I gave while running *The Sinister Secret of Saltmarsh*, an adventure where the party went to investigate strange goings-on at a supposedly haunted manor.[1] Based on that description, do you have a good sense of the imaginary space that the characters are in? What's more, do you feel like you're *there*? Like you're located in that garden before the haunted manor and appraising what actions to take based on what you know about the environment? If you don't, do you think you could suspend your disbelief enough if you tried?

This tumbling into imaginary worlds is why many of us love TTRPGs. We enjoy escaping into fantastical environments and visiting places we could never see with our own eyes, like a haunted manor, an enchanted forest, or the dazzling court of a powerful fey queen. Researchers studying how we interact with media have found that this sense of "being there" can lead to more enjoyment and engagement. For example, one study had subjects play the computer role-playing fantasy game *The Elder Scrolls IV: Oblivion* and then measured both how much players felt transported to the game world and how much they enjoyed playing.[2] They found that the former predicted the latter: the more players felt they were present in the game's fictional land of Cryodiil, the more they enjoyed playing and the more they wanted to explore.

Psychologists call this phenomenon **spatial presence** and define it as a) the feeling of being bodily present in an environment created by a piece of media, and b) feeling you can act in ways that make sense in that environment.[3] Researchers have been studying this concept for decades, starting with how new technology in the 1970s and 1980s—like conference calls and closed-circuit TV—affected perceptions of togetherness. Today, most of the interest in spatial presence is in the context of video games and virtual reality (VR), which seem like they are custom-made to evoke the phenomenon. That said, TTRPG game masters can also create spatial presence for players and players can still help themselves experience that sensation because the theories that explain spatial presence in other media can be used to help us create it in relatively low-tech tabletop games. While TTRPGs haven't yet been addressed in the spatial presence literature, what has been discussed is the so-called "book problem." This is the observation that spatial presence can happen when we read words on a page or hear them read aloud.[4] We can feel present in the worlds created by text that lacks visual, auditory, and other cues because we have imaginations. If text and spoken word count as "media" for the purposes of this research, then it follows that hearing a description of an imaginary space in a TTRPG does too.

One of the most useful theories about the formation of spatial presence comes from an international team of researchers whose model describes a two-step process through which media users experience spatial presence.[5] First, media users construct a mental representation of the imaginary environment or space. Then they adopt that imaginary environment as the primary reference point for where they are. A lot goes into making each of those steps more likely to happen, so let's look at the process in more detail with an eye toward factors most relevant to *Dungeons & Dragons* players.

STEP 1: BUILD A MENTAL MODEL OF THE DUNGEON

Before you can feel present in an imaginary manor, castle, lair, or mine, you must first get your head around what that space is. You have to form what psychologists call **a "mental model" of the environment**.[6] This is an idea about the space's dimensions, its features, what senses it engages, and what it would be like to move around and act in it. This involves allocating attention, perceiving cues about the nature of the space, and pulling in your memories and knowledge to fill in the blanks.

Perceptual Cues

It may seem obvious, but it's worth noting that before you can form a mental model of an imaginary space, you must pay attention to the source of information about that space. This can be involuntary or voluntary. We often involuntarily orient ourselves toward a piece of media when something big or attention-grabbing intrudes on our perceptions like an explosion, a sudden motion, a jarring change of scene, or screaming. In the case of tabletop role-playing games, something as simple as saying a player or character's name will frequently yank their attention back to the game. This is why it's a good idea for game masters to drop in questions such as, "Hey Anisha, what does your character think of this situation?" to reclaim players' attention. "You take 28 necrotic damage," also works in a pinch. In the case of voluntary allocation of attention, TTRPGs have more to offer. Their rich narratives and interactive nature get us to voluntarily pay attention and perceive what's being shared about the imaginary environment.

Once players are paying attention to the media, they can use perceptual cues to create a mental model to help them mentally simulate the environment. These cues come in two broad categories: **spatial cues** from the media and **relevant memories and thoughts** that we bring with us.

Let's talk about spatial cues first. Other types of media use many kinds of spatial cues to literally draw out their imaginary environments. Even something as ancient as lines that converge at a vanishing point create the illusion of looking down a three-dimensional corridor. Early 2D video games used parallax scrolling to make the background scroll more slowly so it appeared to be far away. Movies and television offer surround sound. Virtual reality goes further, offering multiple channels of input for our visual, auditory, tactile, and vestibular senses. That's important because research has shown that the more senses that are engaged by a piece of media and the more verisimilitude with which it does it, the better the resulting mental model of the space.[7] Psychologists use the term **immersion** to refer to the degree to which a virtual environment saturates a media user's perceptual systems.[8] Seeing a picture of a dragon, for example, leads to low immersion. But a person in VR will have a highly immersive experience if they see a dragon approaching, hear its roar, feel the ground tremble, and move their head to track the beast's flight overhead. It's also noteworthy that these spatial cues are most effective when they work in tandem and remain consistent throughout the experience.[9]

TTRPGs can't provide as many spatial cues, but here are some actions game masters can take to engage our senses and offer building blocks for imaginary spaces:

- Use battle maps and minis/tokens to show the dimensions of the environment from an overhead view and be sure to describe features or objects not explicitly shown by the map.
- Provide illustrations to show players what spaces and their contents look like.
- Use music (good) or sound effects (even better) to add ambiance.
- Set up mood lighting by dimming lights to evoke the dankness of a dungeon or use colored lights to imitate a pillar of purple, eldritch energy.
- And, of course, use the power of your own words to help players mentally simulate spaces and all the sounds, sights, textures, movements, and other perceptual cues.

Players can also step up and take control of some of these recommendations to allow game masters to focus on other tasks. As a player, you can volunteer to be in charge of music, lighting, and sound effects based on what the game master requests at the moment. Even beyond this, there's a lot more that players bring to the table, which we'll talk about next.

Relevant Memories and Cognitions

No matter how many rich spatial cues a piece of media or an experience provides, there will always be corners left unfilled. Even with movies, TV, or video games, we only see what the camera shows us and the senses of smell, taste, and touch don't get tapped at all. Media like tabletop role-playing games have even more blank spaces in need of filling. But don't fear, because you can fill in those empty corners of the virtual space with your own memories, thoughts, and knowledge like icing on the cake.[10] For example, fans of classic Western movies who have been to the American Southwest can imagine the baking heat of the desert and the sound of wind rustling through the dry, meager scrub. They can remember the awesome sense of vast, open skies that spatial cues from video cannot fully convey. The same goes for how someone asked to imagine swimming in the ocean will likely imagine the taste of saltwater. Or how someone reading about a lost hiker can get a lot out of thinking about the oppressive, disorienting closeness of the woods they felt during their last hike. You bring in your own memories, assumptions, and familiarity with the imaginary space and use them to simulate it.[11]

This is the main way that mental models are created when simply reading about an imaginary space, and they work with tabletop role-playing games, as well. Here are some actions game masters can take to help players apply their own memories, knowledge, and internal logic when building a model of an imaginary space:

- Describe places by familiar names when appropriate; describe a space as a barracks, a kitchen, a town hall,

a prison, a mine, or whatever else players are familiar with.
- Similarly, don't be afraid to use real-world analogs if they would help; describe a town as "laid out like a college campus" or "set up like a county fair."
- Directly evoke tropes, ideas, or even cliches from a given piece of media if you think it provides the right building blocks; describe something as "much like what Frodo and Sam saw in Tolkien's Mordor" or "the streets are flooded, like in news footage about the aftermath of a hurricane."
- Above all, be willing to change your description of the imaginary space to accommodate assumptions and ideas that players bring; if they seem to assume that there are stables in a castle courtyard or a bard performing in a tavern, make it so.

Players also have responsibilities when bringing their own crafting materials to the building site of an imaginary world. Here are a few actions you can take as a player to create that rich mental model:

- Simulate the space by thinking about how it would operate and what similarities it has to spaces you're familiar with.
- Don't be afraid to ask questions about the imaginary space based on your assumptions and familiarity; if you think it would make sense for there to be a ladder providing access to high ground, ask about it.
- Even better, make declarations about what your character is doing based on your assumptions about the space such as, "I find a game of cards to join at the tavern" or, "I approach the biggest, fanciest looking stall in the marketplace."

When it comes to creating spatial presence, the greatest advantage tabletop role-playing games have over any other media is that their spaces are immediately changeable with a little imagination or a few swipes from a wet-erase marker. I know I've fallen into the trap of assuming that if it's not shown on the map, it's not there, even when it would make sense to inject some interesting possibilities. Game masters can fall into this rut as well, especially when working with published adventures or using pre-existing maps. For the sake of spatial presence, permit yourself to make changes to an imaginary space. Add a staircase to access that balcony. Acknowledge that the din of nearby machinery would make it hard for characters to hear. Ask if there's a back door used for deliveries. Roll with it.

That said, sometimes people are better equipped when they set out to create mental models of imaginary spaces, even relative to others with the same spatial cues and the same experiences to draw from. They're simply better at it.

STEP 2: FROM MENTAL MODELS TO SPATIAL PRESENCE

Spatial presence happens only after two things are accomplished: the first, discussed in the previous section, is developing a mental model of the imaginary space. But experiencing spatial presence also requires that we accept the imaginary space as our primary reference point for where we are located. We must choose to say "yes" in response to the question, "Am I there?"

Some aspects of a typical *Dungeons & Dragons* game help us get to "yes" on this question, such as a strong narrative, characters we love or hate, and a feeling that we can impact the story.[12] But other aspects can easily intrude on our thoughts and push us towards a "no." We may decide that we can't overlook all the inconsistencies reminding us that this is all imaginary. It's possible to make one too many Monty Python references that pull people out of the moment. Or we may not be enjoying the game and thus be unmotivated to feel spatially present. But this second step of choosing to feel spatially present in a make-believe world is where *Dungeons & Dragons* can outshine other types of media.

Involvement

Ever felt so engrossed in a fictional world that you can't stop thinking about it? Like ruminating about how its rules of magic work or what the characters from that world would do in different situations? Ever gobbled up all the lore you could for a campaign setting or story? If so, you've felt **involvement**, one of the most important things we can do to feel like we're present in an imaginary space. Involvement is defined as active, high-level engagement with a piece of media that involves higher-order cognitions and information processing.[13] It's thinking intensely about an imaginary space, interpreting what's going on in it, pondering what it means, and assigning relevance or connection to your own experiences. The more involved you are with a piece of media, the more likely you are to be able to think of yourself as present in the environment. This can include both cognitive components like the ones described above, but it can also include behavioral aspects like taking notes, sketching maps, creating fan art, or even talking to other people about the fictional world.

In addition to these cognitive and behavioral aspects, the emotions evoked by becoming involved with media can also lead to spatial presence. One study had two groups of subjects navigate an ancient Mayan temple recreated in the *Quake 3* video game engine.[14] The control group got a well-lit and static version of the temple to explore. For the experimental group, emotional involvement was enhanced by creating a spooky version of the virtual environment using lighting, weather effects, sound effects, and the sounds of howling monsters. The researchers also gilded the lily a bit by having an off-screen narrator announce, "You are at the entrance of an abandoned temple. Legend has it that one still can find gold in here. But be careful! Legend has it that no one who went in looking for gold ever came back. Huahahahaha!"[15] A bit corny? Yes. Effective? Also yes. Those in the experimental condition reported feeling stronger emotions and more involvement as they went through the abandoned temple. As a result, more of them reported feeling like they could imagine themselves as physically present in the world on the other side of the screen.

It's also the case that people who are interested in the idea of exploring ancient temples would have had an even easier time experiencing spatial presence in this study. Similar to how superfans of H. P. Lovecraft's fiction find it easy to think about and stay interested in the *Call of Cthulhu* role-playing game. Psychologists studying presence call this **domain-specific interest,** and the same study described above about the ancient Mayan temples found a link between people's interest in the topic and their motivation to get cognitively and emotionally involved.

TTRPGs are better suited to involvement than any other media because of their interactive, narrative nature. Given this, there are ways to become more involved as a player. Something to keep in mind is that involvement is voluntary. It happens when we choose to think deeply about a piece of media, to explore its emotional implications, and to ponder what it means for the characters in play. So do that! If you need some concrete suggestions, consider these:

- Be the party note-taker, which requires involvement in the form of committing things to memory, recording

them in ways that are accessible to others, connecting ideas, and making inferences about meaning.
- Engage in role-playing in a way that makes sense for your character in that environment.
- Relatedly, get creative with your combat and exploration actions in ways that require thinking about the environment in detail.
- Describe your character's interactions with the environment in a similarly detailed way.
- Especially if you're the game master, find out your players' domain-specific interests in themes, tones, settings, and whatever else you can reasonably incorporate into the game.

Suspension of Disbelief

Finally, sometimes the biggest barrier to accepting the idea that we are present in an imaginary world is that the real world makes too compelling a case to the contrary. Distractions from the real world can intrude on our efforts to be spatially present. Game rules for overland travel seem arbitrary and weird. The way that the world operates in the imaginary space doesn't make sense and we're unsatisfied with the game master's explanation of "I dunno, *magic*." In these kinds of situations, we can choose to force ourselves into feeling like we're present in an imaginary world by taking a deep breath and lifting with our legs as we engage in **suspension of disbelief**.[16]

Borrowing from literature theory, researchers investigating spatial presence have found that certain people are willing and able to suspend disbelief by ignoring what doesn't make sense about an imaginary world, tuning out distractions from the real world, and silencing the thought that "this is just a game." If you've ever "turned off your brain" so that you could lean back and enjoy a summer blockbuster movie, then you've done something similar. If all else fails, ignore the thoughts that try to bubble up whenever you want to sink into the game world and experience it as if you were there. Reality can wait until the game session is done!

All of this said, it's true that not everyone *wants* to experience spatial presence. I have played in campaigns where everyone wants to treat the game as an exercise in tactical combat. In those games, everything you're going to get about an imaginary space is described in terms of 5-by-5 squares and combat rules. In this case, most likely, the game master will deliver the game's story like they're reciting a Wikipedia entry—if there's a story at all. And that's fine if that's what everyone wants! A lot of people play *Dungeons & Dragons* like that and have a good time. But for those of us who want to feel like we're setting foot in an imaginary world, understanding the psychology behind spatial presence in other kinds of media can help us take that approach to the game.

Now that we have explored some of the features of *Dungeons & Dragons* that can lead to deeper enjoyment and satisfaction, let's take a step outside of the experience of playing the game and let's talk about the psychology of all the *stuff* that players collect to make those experiences happen. And why those collections can be so psychologically meaningful.

WHAT YOU LEARNED IN THIS CHAPTER

- Spatial presence is the feeling that you are physically located in an imagined space and able to act within it.
- Spatial presence happens after players do two things:
  - First, create a detailed mental model of the imaginary space.
  - Second, accept that they are physically present in the imagined environment instead of the real world.
- The creation of mental models of a space is facilitated by spatial cues such as images, sounds, and other sensory inputs.
- The more sensory inputs there are, the more vivid those inputs are, and the more they work in tandem, the better.
- Immersion is the degree to which a media user's different senses are flooded with rich input.
- Players also bring their own relevant personal memories and cognitions to the experience so that they can fill in the gaps in their mental model.
- Once a rich mental model is created, players wishing to experience spatial presence must accept the idea that they are present there.
- Involvement, which is active, voluntary, and high-level engagement with a piece of media, greatly helps players feel presence once a mental model of a space is created.
- Involvement is aided by players' specific interests or attraction to whatever themes, tones, styles, and experiences the game is offering.

- Players can choose to suspend disbelief about being present in a fictional space.
- Experiencing spatial presence in this way has been shown to lead to higher enjoyment of different kinds of media.

HOW TO APPLY THIS CHAPTER TO YOUR GAME

- If you're a game master, provide as many perceptual cues about the environment as you can through detailed descriptions, sound effects, lighting, and visual aids.
- If you're a player, focus your attention on these cues and the game in general while trying to minimize outside distractions that remind you about the world outside of the game.
- Strive to experience involvement by thinking about the game, its world, the narrative it presents, its themes, its lore, and whatever else captures your imagination.
- When possible, game masters should try to tailor experiences to the interests of the players both so that they can create their rich mental model of the world and maintain involvement with it.

CHAPTER 5

WHY DO SOME PLAYERS HOARD STUFF LIKE THEY'RE DRAGONS?

Do you have enough dice in your gaming collection? That's a trick question. The answer is "no" because you can never have enough dice. If someone tells you otherwise, show them all the dice you don't yet own and demand that they explain themselves. Alex Kammer probably knows this, though his collection of *Dungeons & Dragons* artifacts is famous for being more than a gigantic bowl full of dice. Much more. Kammer, an affable, middle-aged attorney working in Wisconsin, is living the life that many *Dungeons & Dragons* collectors dream of. He runs games with both long-time friends and gaming industry luminaries from what he calls "the Gamehole," a room that's part gaming space and part museum. When he plays, he sits under the original, hand-drawn map of The Forgotten Realms, the default campaign setting for recent editions of *Dungeons & Dragons*. The map found its way from legendary creator Ed Greenwood to Kammer by a circuitous route that Kammer happily retraced for me in a video conference call. Thousands of such artifacts of gaming history surround players in Kammer's games, including bookshelves full of modules, rulebooks, accessories, and boxed sets both mundane and rare. Kammer's claim to fame among collectors is that he has at least one copy—in original shrink-wrap—of every *Dungeons & Dragons* product put out by its original publisher, TSR. This part of his collection starts with the first printing of 1971's *Chainmail: Rules for Medieval Miniatures*, the immediate precursor to the original edition of *Dungeons & Dragons,* up through the last TSR publication in 2000.[1]

As if that wasn't enough, the Gamehole, along with the rest of Kammer's house, sits above a pub that he owns. Plus he has parlayed his love of *Dungeons of Dragons* into running a successful annual gaming convention called Gamehole Con in tribute to the repository for his collection. "It's a pretty nice little tree house," he laughed as he waved his webcam around so I could see from my end of the call. "It's what I wanted when I was twelve."[2]

When I asked Kammer why he started the collection, he shrugged and said that it was part of his personality. He bought his first *Advanced Dungeons & Dragons Player's Handbook* from the Value Village department store sometime in the late 1970s and took meticulous care of it just like all his other belongings. "I was the kind of kid who printed his name neatly in the corner of the book and took care of them," he said. "I never dog-eared the pages, always kept things on shelves and in drawers." His collection of *Dungeons & Dragons* books grew, but he stepped away from the hobby when we left home to attend college and law school. Eventually, as an adult, Kammer told me he came back to the game in the 1990s and realized that there was so much he had missed. He also realized that he was, in his words, "a completionist nerd" and at this point, he had a lot more disposable income than he did as a kid. So he kicked off his new collection of TSR-published *Dungeons & Dragons* products with a stack of 50 shrink-wrapped adventure modules that he bought from another collector. According to Kammer, his collection was finally completed in the summer of 2022.

I find collectors like Alex Kammer fascinating, in part because of his "completionist nerd" personality type with a drive to preserve interesting artifacts. He even has separate "reading/playing" and "preservation" copies of many items. But there's a lot more that goes on in the minds of collectors, whether they own every *Dungeons & Dragons* publication or they're just someone who can't help buying one more set of dice, snatching up one more set of miniatures, or preordering every new rulebook once it's announced. Fortunately, if we're looking for answers to why we amass gaming collections like dragons building their hoards, psychology can tell us why certain items appeal to collectors.

ELUSIVENESS

One of my most cherished items is the first edition of the *Deities & Demigods* rulebook, published in 1980. My family was embarking on a summer vacation and I talked my dad into buying it so I would have something to read on the long drive. The book was a guide to the gods, demigods, and heroes from Greek, Chinese, Native American, Sumerian, and many other pantheons. Want to fight Anubis, the Egyptian guardian of the dead? This book has you covered. He has a -2 armor class, 300 hit points, 20 levels of cleric, 12 levels of paladin, and 20 levels of magic-user. (Yeah, early versions of *Dungeons & Dragons* seem weird looking back at them now.) I didn't know it then, but that sly request for vacation reading material netted me what would go on to become a rare collector's item that both Alex Kammer and I have in our collections.

The reason is that people at TSR hadn't done their full due diligence regarding all the intellectual property the book included. Specifically, they hadn't nailed down permission to include deities, monsters, and heroes from the Cthulhu mythos by H. P. Lovecraft and the Melnibonèan mythos featuring characters from fantasy author Michael Moorcock's work.[3] According to *Deities & Demigods* co-author James Ward, TSR thought it had secured permission from the rights holders to include this material, so the first edition of the book went to press in 1980. But the next year they received a cease-and-desist letter from another game publishing company named Chaosium, which claimed that *it* owned the exclusive rights to publish gaming material based on the Lovecraft and Moorcock properties. Both companies initially agreed to a compromise where a special thanks was given to Chaosium in the book's preface, but TSR eventually decided that future printings of *Deities & Demigods* would quietly omit the Lovecraft and Moorcock pages altogether.

But I had a copy from one of the first printings, with the Cthulhu and Elric of Melnibonè in it, and I remain excited about it to this day. If all goes according to plan, I'm going to be buried with it.

One quirk of the human brain that studies have consistently found is that when something is scarce or we think it's about to become scarce, we tend to value it more. The assumption that if something is difficult to get, it's more desirable than something readily available, is one of those well-worn mental shortcuts that offers a great balance between mental effort and accuracy of judgment. Psychologist Stephen Worchel illustrated this with a study involving chocolate chip cookies.[4] Pretending to be doing a consumer products survey, he and his colleagues offered shoppers a cookie from one of two jars. Some were asked to retrieve a cookie from a nearly full jar. Others picked from a jar with only two cookies lying among some crumbs at the bottom. When asked, shoppers reported that the cookies from the mostly empty jars were more delicious, more desirable, and should be more expensive. This is despite the fact that both jars contained the same type of cookies, all of them retrieved from a big box just out of sight. It was the perceived rarity or supply of the cookies and the assumption that someone else had already taken most of them, that made the shoppers think better of them.

We see this all the time in limited run and limited time promotions or collector's editions. Beginning with the 5th edition of *Dungeons & Dragons*, Wizards of the Coast has published versions of its hardback books with alternative covers for collectors. Some of them are striking and beautiful, but the appeal for many is that they were made in limited runs. This means they are much rarer than the normal editions. For example, as I write this, you can buy a copy of the *Ghosts of Saltmarsh* hardback adventure book for under $30 if you want the regular version. Or you can drop $160 if you are set on the version with the alternative cover. The boxed set of the *Player's Handbook, Dungeon Master's Guide,* and *Monster Manual* with alternative covers would cost you $549 if you could find a retailer that has it in stock. Why does the market bear that price? Because just like my copy of the 1st edition of *Deities and Demigods*, everyone knows that only so many of them exist. Things are often valuable simply because they are rare. Alex Kammer's collection, for example, includes a copy of *The Jade Hare*, one of the rarest adventure modules known. Originally available from TSR's mail order service in 1992, only 10 intact copies of the module are known to exist, and only two remain in their original shrink-wrap. Kammer has one of them perched in a place of honor within his "rares" cabinet, along with other scarce oddities.

More to the point, an item only has to be *perceived* as rare to have value, whether it really is scarce or simply because someone is tinkering with our perceptions. Such tinkering can happen when we are made to believe that an item will be made rarer in the future. When a tabletop role-playing game publisher creates a limited run of books, minis, or other accessories, they are creating scarcity and making something more elusive than it has to be. The miniature-making company Wizkids, for example, frequently includes limited, promotional figures that can only be obtained by buying high-price, premium miniatures or cases full of blind boxes from specific retailers. Especially for new products, that rarity is manufactured and exists in the eye of the beholder. Especially if it's the variant edition of the *Monster Manual* with a beholder on the cover.[5] The point is, you don't have to pay more, preorder, or buy from specific retailers to get some limited-edition item if you don't want to.

On the other hand, elusiveness is part of the reason why many people love building collections. They get pleasure from it. Marketing researchers and other experts who have studied why people collect things have found that it's the thrill of the hunt that drives many of them.[6] Some people like scouring used bookstores, online auctions, and dealers' tables at conventions for rarities and treasures. The appeal isn't just owning the rare thing. It's hunting for it, hoping you'll find it, and then finding it—or finding it through serendipity. Alex Kammer told me a story about how he was perusing the dealer area at a small convention in Texas and was thrilled to discover an elusive *Dungeons & Dragons* "trail map." This was a guide to fantastical locations published in limited numbers by TSR in 1989. It was the only one he was missing and there it was, in like-new condition and priced at just a few dollars. If you enjoy hunting for collectibles and you're not emptying your bank account to do it, then do it. Just approach collecting on your own terms, not some marketing plan's terms.

AUTHENTICITY

The thrill of the hunt aside, one wonders why rarity matters at a time when technology makes copying something trivially easy. To answer that, consider one of the items in Alex Kammer's collection that he seemed particularly proud of. "I just paid an absurd amount of money for a 5th printing original *Dungeons & Dragons* white box where all the books were signed by Dave Arneson *and* Gary Gygax," he told me. This pairing of signatures is vanishingly rare because those two co-creators of *Dungeons & Dragons* grew to despise each other to the point where if one signed something, the other would refuse to add their signature.

That's pretty cool, but isn't it just marks on paper? What makes signatures so special? What if a collector of such autographs watched me take one of the signed books, put it in a photocopy machine, press the green button, and then proffer the still warm copy for sale? Would that person pay as much as they would for the original autograph? Would they pay anything? How long until I hear the words "That's him over there, officer" and have to make a break for it?

Of course, nobody would buy my photocopied autograph because it's not the real thing. It's not authentic, which is why original art is more valuable than prints. Similarly, the *Player's Handbook* is the only tome I lost from my childhood collection of original *Advanced Dungeons & Dragons* rulebooks. It disappeared through one of the world's cracks at some point and I haven't been able to find it. I would love to have a complete set of *Advanced Dungeons & Dragons* rulebooks again even though I don't play that version of the game anymore, yet I have not availed myself of a print-on-demand service to replace it with a fresh, near-identical copy. Because it wouldn't be authentic and authenticity matters.[7]

But even if I did buy an authentic copy of the 1978 *Advanced Dungeons & Dragons Player's Handbook*, it still wouldn't be quite the same. Because it wouldn't be *my* copy. Buying from another collector or auction wouldn't make me as content and my collection wouldn't feel as complete as it would if I were to go digging around in old boxes and unearth *my* dog-eared copy. That copy has a history that even another authentic copy would not have.

PSYCHOLOGICAL HISTORY

An object's history doesn't have to be *our* history to enhance its value, though. We often value an object because it used to belong to someone else. Following in the great tradition of examining the obvious, Bruce Hood from the University of Bristol and Paul Bloom from Yale University tested this idea that a copy is seen as different by even the most naïve subjects: children.[8] In their experiment, they lied to children. If that bothers you, know that researchers do this all the time in the name of science. (I don't know if that will make you feel better or worse about the lying, but it's true.) In this case, they showed a bunch of six-year-olds a cup that supposedly belonged to the Queen of England. Very regal. Very impressive. Then they placed the cup in a supposed "duplicating machine" that would make an exact copy of it. In truth, the researchers used a contraption with a trick door they could use to pop in an identical cup. The supposed duplication complete, they then asked the children to assign values to both the original and the copy by asking how much they would have to be paid to give up the original and how much they would be willing to pay for the copy.

Unsurprisingly, even kids with a minimal understanding of money slapped higher price tags on the original cup that had supposedly passed the Queen's lips. That quality, they decided, didn't transfer to the copy just like how a person's pressing pen to paper doesn't transfer to a photocopy of a signature. It makes no sense on the face of it, but we humans commonly imbue objects with an aura, soul, or inexplicable quality transferred from its owner to the object. You can look at it with all the passionless logic you want, but suppose someone offered you either a d20 that had been rolled by superstar game master Matt Mercer during an episode of the popular *Critical Role* show or an identical d20 fresh out of its box from the local game shop. We both know you'd want the first one. Similarly, at the literal center of Alex Kammer's eclectic Gamehole collection is a gaming table that was once owned by famous game designer Monte Cook, who is known for writing and helping design earlier versions of *Dungeons & Dragons*. It looks like any other table, but its history makes you say, "Oh, cool!" when he tells you about it.

One group of researchers showed the importance of psychological history by measuring people's willingness to purchase an ordinary-looking sweater.[9] Shoppers were willing to spend more if it was a sweater owned by a celebrity they admired, and they were ready to spend even more if the celebrity reportedly wore the sweater frequently. We feel that the person's essence is contagious and can spread to the objects they interact with. This is the second reason why my photocopied autographs by Dave Arneson and Gary Gygax would be worthless; they're not only unauthentic, the paper never came into contact with the famed game designers. Interestingly, this contagion concept lowers value when applied to celebrities who are more infamous than famous. Joseph Stalin's 3rd edition *Dungeons & Dragons* character sheet (a gnome bard named "Fiddles McGee," weirdly enough) should sell for less than character sheets belonging to most other equally famous historical figures.

POSSESSIONS AS EXTENSIONS OF OURSELVES

People don't collect or hang onto things only because they're rare, authentic, or have a history. Why, for example, do people buy every official *Dungeons & Dragons* rulebook and put dragon-shaped hunks of plastic on their birthday gift wish lists? Besides their obvious functions for playing the game, we often build these collections as a way of extending ourselves and making ourselves more understandable to others.[10] Like hobbies, collections make our interests, our passions, and our values evident to others in a concrete (or, rather, plastic and paper) way that sets us apart from some people and places us in the company of others. When we have someone over and show them our collection or when we display it conspicuously behind us during video conference calls, it communicates something about us that we want others to know. That we're creative, imaginative, social, a lover of games, and maybe, if we're honest about it, that we have the money to spend on stuff like obsidian dice and enormous models of Tiamat, Queen of Evil Dragons. Curated collections send a much stronger, more focused message about who we are than everyday possessions like groceries, furniture, or clothes because they speak to the time, effort, and thought put into acquiring them.

So yeah. You need more dice.

THINGS YOU LEARNED IN THIS CHAPTER

- The knowledge that something is scarce or about to become scarce can greatly impact our estimation of how valuable or desirable it is.
- Authenticity matters to collections and collectors. A copy of something might be worth having, but all else being equal, an original is always a more desirable addition to a collection.
- An object's history can make it more valuable, too. We often hang on to things because they evoke nostalgia or similar emotions.
- We often consider an object's previous owner or history. The experience of being close to or related to someone else feels like it can transfer to us through the possession of an object.
- People often use collections as a form of self-expression and an extension of parts of their identity. They serve as signals to other people and ways to find people like us.

PART II
PLAYING THE GAME

CHAPTER 6
WHY AND HOW DO WE IDENTIFY WITH OUR IN-GAME CHARACTERS?

The earliest progenitors of *Dungeons & Dragons* never expected you to think much about your character's thoughts, feelings, or worldview. They never expected you to play as a brooding, halfling wizard, much less develop an elaborate backstory for her. They never expected you to think, "What would *this character* do?" when deciding how to interact with others. Expectations around character interactions were sharply limited. If an average pre-TTRPG player time-traveled from the 1960s to your gaming table today, he would be mystified and probably a little put off by the story-driven, character-centric, role-play heavy games we play today.

Eventually, the culture around *Dungeons & Dragons* shifted to value role-play, but the path to get here was a long and circuitous one. In his exhaustive history of tabletop games *Playing at the World: A History of Simulating Wars, People, and Fantastic Adventures from Chess to Role-Playing Games*, Jon Peterson takes us on an extended hike along that road.[1] In the first few miles, during the 1950s and 1960s, we find scattered pockets of nerdy weirdos obsessing over recreations of historical battles fought with tiny metal soldiers and other literal toys. These sound a lot like playing with the plastic miniatures and tokens we use in TTRPG games today, but there was one fundamental difference: wargaming figures from those days had a many-to-one representation, as opposed to one-to-one. That is, a single figure might represent an entire group of 20 musketeers instead of a single person like in modern role-playing games. In some battlefield recreations, a single figure stood in for as many as 100 soldiers. Enthusiasts eventually began to "individuate" (Jon Peterson's word and I love it) particular minis, referring to them as veterans with special abilities that set them apart from others. In a society with limited mass media (much less the internet and social media), these ideas and enhancements were promulgated mainly through wargaming fanzines and conventions. But within a few years, players were giving names and personal characteristics to their veteran units and adopting the one-to-one representation for minis that we find familiar today. Noted one player in a 1953 wargaming newsletter, "I love to pour individuality into my characters; Corporal Sebastian Gridiron suffers from bunions."[2] Giving poor Corporal Gridiron bunions was more prescient than anyone knew because soon systems for naming and tracking individual members of companies, platoons, phalanxes, and other groups of soldiers became popular. So much so that one 1966 newsletter article entitled "Humanizing the Roster System" became widely shared for its method of tracking the names, ranks, and attributes of particular soldiers.[3]

This idea of using a character sheet to track individual characteristics continued to evolve, though the contents of the sheets didn't always correspond to people. Early naval games, for example, had individual ship statistics tracked on cards reminiscent of character sheets. Later, though, the concept was applied to people. A 1970 Wild West simulation game called *Western Gunfight Wargame Rules* not only had players represent their single character with a single miniature, but it also had them choose different skills (e.g., hand-to-hand, rifle) and different equipment (e.g., knife, repeating rifle) among other individuating qualities.

WHY AND HOW DO WE IDENTIFY WITH OUR IN-GAME CHARACTERS?

All these choices were written down on a "record sheet" that carried over from game to game.[4]

But this still wasn't role-playing as we currently think about it. If players were affecting drawls and donning cowboy hats as they played *Western Gunfight*, it wasn't codified in the rules. That practice began to change a little in 1971 when Gary Gygax and his wargaming pal Jeff Perrin released *Chainmail: Rules for Medieval Miniatures*, which you may remember as the most immediate predecessor of *Dungeons & Dragons*. *Chainmail* focused on using miniatures to simulate man-on-man combat, except in the "fantasy supplement" half of the book, which threw in fantastical opponents like hobbits, dwarves, heroes, wizards, trolls, wraiths, and one guy named Steve, if I'm reading this low-res scan of the original rules correctly. I may not be. But there was one thing that *Chainmail's* focus on battlefield settings was missing: dungeons. At least until another huge wargaming nerd decided to fix that.

Dave Arneson, another friend of Gygax, loved *Chainmail* and decided to adapt his own existing "Blackmoor" campaign to it. Arneson, however, decided on a more character-centric experience. In his games, players left the sprawling battlefields to have their individual characters fight their way through labyrinthine, underground complexes in search of heroic deeds and loads of treasure in order to level up. It's in surviving documents from Blackmoor that we can see some of the clearest evidence for the popularization of role-playing games. One character sheet for "The Wizard Gaylord" lists many qualities of the eponymous magic-user that have nothing to do with his functions as a wargaming unit. Gaylord had scores from 1 to 14 in attributes like Brains, Courage, Credibility, and Sex (you go, Gaylord). It was, in the words of Jon Peterson, "a system for more than just a wargaming unit: it aspires to be a system for simulating a person."[5]

So energizing was this concept of holistically simulating a person that Gygax and Arneson leaned into it and published the first edition of *Dungeons & Dragons* in 1974. And yet, despite this clear trend towards more individuated characters, the term "role-playing" never appears in this first edition of the game. Still, the trajectory was set and people were into the general concept. Each subsequent edition of *Dungeons & Dragons* introduced more elements to help players create personal tales, devise campaign hooks that involve characters' backstories, and intentionally step inside fictional characters' minds when deciding what to say and do within the game. You should use that accent, later editions implied. Type out that backstory. Choose some character flaws. The game experience will be much richer with more personal stories, you'll have more investment in the game's outcomes, and moments will be made more memorable because they were specific to your character.

That's the conventional wisdom, at any rate. But how exactly do we get into the heads of our characters and identify with them? What makes them feel like real people instead of little wargaming units? What can we get out of experimenting with different identities through role-playing? And what are some of the consequences of dreaming up a detailed character and then enthusiastically hopping into their head?

EXPERIMENTING WITH SOCIAL ROLES

One thing people often describe when I ask them why they enjoy *Dungeons & Dragons* is that it provides them with a chance to experiment with being other people without worrying about judgment or damage to their reputation. Maybe they don't use those specific words, but the idea is the same. Specifically, players get to take on the perspective of a character whose situation and outlook differ fundamentally from their own. Sometimes it's hard to know what we think of someone until we pretend to be someone else deciding what they think of them. Or even just pretend to *be* that person ourselves. In one survey of 161 tabletop role-playing gamers, 88% of respondents agreed with the statement, "It is easy to experiment with different social roles in role-playing" and many of them specifically mentioned doing so to improve their social skills, develop empathy for others, and explore their own identity.[6] Said one respondent to that survey, "I've taught myself to relate to other people by attempting to see life from different points of view. I think it's because of this that I'm not completely obnoxious today."

Players such as this may want to play at being a disenfranchised gutter rat trying to survive in a system where the cards are stacked against them. Or they may want to play at being a bored noble for whom everything in life has been a breeze so far. Or a deeply religious acolyte with a sunny disposition and unshakable faith. Or a hulking, snaggletooth orc of indeterminate gender who solves problems through the power of friendship and/or unspeakable violence. This activity where you try to imagine and understand the mental state of another person, fictional or real, is called **perspective-taking,** and it has been studied by psychology researchers for decades to understand how we navigate the difficulties of complex social landscapes.[7] It is a psychological skill that starts showing up at around age five when we begin to understand that other people have minds distinct from our own, a milestone known as developing a **theory of mind**.[8] It's a big shift and one of the reasons why young kids can be so annoying. Once they get the idea that other people exist independently and have their own opinions, emotions, and viewpoints, everything changes because if you can comprehend the minds of others, you can understand how to get along with them. You can figure out how to exploit them. Or you can relate to them or do anything else you want to in a social context. It's one of humanity's superpowers.

To understand the mind of another person, it helps to put a bit of effort into thinking like them. Perspective-taking is a deliberate act where you observe another person (or even just hear about them) and ponder their mental state. What are they thinking, feeling, and going through? What's their history? How do they see the world? What are their biases and assumptions? Research has shown that when we do this, we tend to develop more positive attitudes towards the other person and even the social groups that we see them as members of. One study, for example, looked at the adjectives people used to describe a person whose perspective they had taken on and found that trying to see things through the eyes of others increased the overlap in the words used to describe one's self and words used to describe the other person.[9] Take on another's perspective and you'll assume that you have more things in common with them. Another bit of research had fans of the *Game of Thrones* TV show undergo magnetic resonance imaging of their brains. The researchers found that thinking about the *Game of Thrones* characters that they identified with coincided with activity in parts of the brain used to think about and represent knowledge of the self.[10] Interestingly, this was less true when thinking about characters they said they *did not* identify with. In both of these studies and others like them, researchers argue that participants started to blend their identity with that of the other person when they took on their perspective.

This kind of perspective-taking also works to undermine unconscious habits of maintaining stereotypes against others. This is especially true if we see them as members of social groups outside of our own, such as categories defined by race, gender, ability, or class. Not only are we more likely to approach and exhibit friendly behaviors towards the other person if we try to take on their perspective, but we are also less likely to work at maintaining whatever stereotypes might influence our thinking and even become more likely to acknowledge that we possess such unconscious biases.[11] People who try to take on another's perspective also tend to be less likely to fall for a cognitive error known as the **fundamental attribution error**. Falling prey to this error happens when we attribute someone's actions to their more innate qualities rather than environmental and situational causes. We may think, for example, that someone lashed out because they are inherently belligerent, not because they were exhausted from a long day of work. We also tend to do the opposite when explaining our actions by emphasizing the importance of personal qualities and underemphasizing situational explanations. When we strive to take on the perspective of another, we start attributing their behaviors in ways more in line with how we would explain our own.

Perspective-taking, then, is a powerful tool for understanding your character, thinking like them, and playing at being someone you can't be outside of the game. I have my own experience with this. I once played Parsnip, a goblin artificer snatched from the machines-and-magic world of Eberron and pitted against an oppressive tyrant in the gothic horror adventure, *Curse of Strahd*. Back home at the university where he used to tinker with his creations, Parsnip was a goblin fighting to succeed in a human-dominated world that didn't think much of his species. I took that perspective when role-playing Parsnip, making him habitually work to fit in and try to impress others while holding a grudge against those who got in his way. Ultimately, when the villain who lived in Castle Ravenloft was defeated, I had Parsnip decide that he would rather stay and rule over the campaign's gloomy world than return to his life in Eberon. Am I, the player, now free of all subconscious bias and stereotyping because of a little role-playing? No, undoubtedly not; it's not that easy. But it was an interesting, memorable exercise in perspective-taking.

My point is that many players seize the chance to role-play characters when games like *Dungeons & Dragons* give them the opportunity because doing so lets them play around with new perspectives. If we try to take on those characters' points of view, we will not only like the characters more and find more in common with them, but we can develop empathy and kinder attitudes towards members of outgroups. Of course, you'll only be able to take this concept so far in practice when dreaming up your character's hardships and emotions. Your tablemates might reasonably not want to play in a game world flush with overt racism, sexual violence, or other societal shortcomings imported from the real world. But you can always work to set up allegories and approximations. You can always explore other, less traumatic ways that your character differs from you. You'll know and remember that character better as a result.

PLAYER FRAMES

Gary Allen Fine is a sociologist whose interests encompass many groups that seem distant from one another. Subjects of his many studies include mushroom hunters, Little League baseball players, and *Dungeons & Dragons* fans. Fine was, in fact, one of the first academics to seriously study the effects of TTRPGs on players during the 1980s. Based on his observations, he believed that players engaged with such games through one of three frames at any given moment:
1. The frame of the real world
2. The frame of the game system
3. The frame of the player character within the game[12]

WHY AND HOW DO WE IDENTIFY WITH OUR IN-GAME CHARACTERS?

The first frame, that of the real world, is one that we're all hopefully familiar with. It's knowing where you are and that you're a person sitting in a room with other people (or connected online, if that's the case). When players say, "I'm having fun," or "I forgot my dice," or "Pass the pizza," this is the frame they're operating in. It's the default frame for experiencing the world and the one we spend most of our days in.

The second frame deals with the game system. It's understanding the game's rules, its expectations, and its tools, like the dice or minis that are used to play. When a player calculates remaining movement, ponders the effects of a Polymorph spell, or thinks about how to level up their character, they are viewing the experience through this second frame. To the extent that everyone can operate within this same frame, it creates **the magic circle**, which is a shared understanding that everyone is playing a game with its own sets of rules and expectations that only apply within that circle of activity and agreement.

Fine's third frame involves being able to see the world through the eyes of one's character. It's the most relevant to this chapter and it's the most unwieldy and difficult one for a lot of people. This is because it requires the player to think as a fictitious character would think and ponder how that character would make sense of the world. In many ways, it's the role-playing frame. When a mild-mannered player decides to have his barbarian character fly into a rage in the face of a minor insult, that's viewing the world through the third frame.

It's worth noting that players slip and slide between these frames constantly and with little friction. Sometimes in the same breath. A player might say, for example, "Melcurio wants to avoid violence so he tries to convince the guard to let him pass. Can I borrow a d20? Thanks. Okay, I rolled an 18 for my Persuasion check." In this one quick series of utterances, the player first operated in frame 3 (saying what his character does and why), then frame 1 (asking a fellow player if he can borrow a die), then frame 2 (stating an outcome in the context of the game's mechanics). Fine argued that this kind of fluidity is necessary for all the players to have a shared gaming experience and that things break down if a player can't access one of the frames or move between them.[13] This might be a useful context for players and game masters for separating and compartmentalizing their thoughts about their friends, the game system, and their characters. Of course, sometimes those barriers are more porous than we'd like.

 BLEED

While players might come to identify with their characters through role-play and perspective-taking, all but the most dedicated method actors recognize that the player and the character are two separate identities, starkly divided. Deep immersion into the game and one's character can poke momentary holes in the barrier between players and characters, however, and gaming scholars have observed thoughts, emotions, motivations, and attitudes that seep through from one identity to the other. Some of these theorists have gone so far as to claim that particularly immersed players may go beyond the concept of perspective-taking to the point where they fully experience another person or character by taking on their emotions, internal states, and motivations as if they were their own.[14] These players may experience a kind of doubled-up consciousness or "ironic imagination" in which they experience reality from multiple frames of reference without thinking it weird.[15] The identity of their character exists alongside their own and they think about them both.

This is far out there, but **bleed** is the term given to a milder version of this permeation of the line between self and character,[16] and there are a few different types. **Bleed-in** occurs when a player's attitudes or emotions drive what a character does or supposedly feels. Are you annoyed with your friend for criticizing how you're playing the game and as a result your character acts short-tempered with their character? That's bleed-in. **Bleed-out** follows the opposite path: a character's actions or attitudes affect a player's mental state outside of the game. If you glower across the table at another player and grab the last piece of pizza after their character steals more than their fair share of the loot, that's bleed-out. Both types of bleed are subconscious, but the phenomenon known as **steering** occurs when a player *consciously* guides their character's actions for out-of-game reasons related to their mental state.[17] If you're feeling flirty towards a fellow player sitting next to you, you could have your character interact more with his character and ply the character with gifts.

Whether bleed and steering are good or bad phenomena is somewhat a matter of perspective. Some players enjoy reacting to their characters' situations with real emotion, for example. Some players might use steering as a way to safely explore their own emotions or thoughts. But any of us who have said something and then had the game master ask, "Wait, is that what your character says?" knows that it can sometimes work against the role-playing. Furthermore, if your goal is to take on the perspective and internal state of your character, having your own emotions or thoughts steer the character's in-game behavior is counter to that. So be aware of these phenomena when you play and strike the right balance between identifying closely with your character and keeping enough space between the two of you so that you don't double up on the personality.

WHAT YOU LEARNED IN THIS CHAPTER

- The wargaming precursors to *Dungeons & Dragons* didn't have players take on roles of individuals, but that concept slowly evolved and culminated with modern role-playing game design.
- For many people, one of the appeals of role-playing games is experimenting with different identities in a safe, encouraging context.
- Theory of mind is a concept describing the developmental milestone where we come to realize that minds other than our own exist and that we can understand or manipulate them.
- Perspective-taking is the conscious process of trying to figure out what another person—real or fictive—is thinking, feeling, and sensing.
- Perspective-taking can create feelings of similarity to the target person, as well as undermine stereotyping and make you more receptive to them.
- Players move between three frames or perspectives when playing: that of the real world, that of the game system, and that of their character.
- High immersion into a character can lead to bleed, which is where your identity as a player impacts what your character does, or vice-versa.
- Steering happens when you consciously guide your character's actions for out-of-game reasons.

HOW TO APPLY THIS CHAPTER TO YOUR GAME

- Engage in perspective-taking for your characters by asking yourself what they may be thinking, feeling, and doing in response to what's going on so that you can simulate their mental state in your head.
- Avoid the fundamental attribution error by thinking about how environmental or social factors could influence your character's behavior, as opposed to their internal traits.
- Think about what you and your character have in common to create more overlap between your identities and feel closer to them.
- Generally, try to avoid bleed-in, bleed-out, and steering, where your mental states and those of your characters start to influence one another.

CHAPTER 7

WHAT GETS US TO ROLE-PLAY AND WHY SHOULD WE CARE?

Now that you understand the benefits (and possibly the downsides) of identifying with your character, let's discuss how to make that role-playing happen. Players in one *Dungeons & Dragons* game I ran got into the campaign and their characters in a big way. In it, the party was whisked away to the Feywild, a place of whimsical magic and strange creatures inspired by classic fairy tales. In response, the players leaned into the inherent theatrics and playfulness of this adventure with a little help from their home wardrobe. One of them played a bard who looked like he just stepped off the stage at a 1980s hair metal show, so the player wore a spiky wig and brought an electric guitar to the table. He played a quick riff whenever his character cast a spell. Another player wore bunny ears plucked from his kid's Easter basket because his character was a harengon, a race of rabbit-like people. Another player wore a pair of plastic horns like those sprouting from the forehead of his tiefling character. It was all pretty great.

And, honestly, these players aren't even that extreme. Many of the popular "actual play" shows on YouTube or Twitch.tv lean into dress-up and props even further, wearing elaborate makeup and costumes as part of their role-playing performance. It's often an amazing confluence of cosplay and tabletop role-playing games accompanied by other types of theatrics, such as acting for the camera and riffing off of other characters. The players take on nonverbal behaviors like modulating their voice or using body language to act out fear, indignation, gratitude, amazement, or any of the hundreds of emotions that their character may be feeling. And while acting out large, physical motions to mimic swinging a sword or running through a forest is hard to do at a table, players often do what they can and let imagination fill in the rest. The rest of us don't have to go quite as far as those performing for a webcam, but multiple lines of psychology research suggest that even wearing Halloween store pointy ears and brandishing a broom handle like an axe can help us embody those items and their symbolic meaning to engage in more immersive role-play, if we feel safe from embarrassment and assume everyone is there for a good time, that is.

PRETEND PLAY, ROLE-PLAY

One of the earliest social skills we develop as children is play. It starts pretty simply, with basic activities that let us get our heads around the world's physics settings. Things get more relevant to our purposes in this chapter when we start to do what's called pretend play. During this activity, we combine play and pretense by imagining that things are not the way they are and then running with whatever idea comes to mind. It is, in a way, stretching our imagined reality so that it fits, snugly or loosely, over the real world.[1] That chair isn't a chair, it's a horse. This mound of dirt is a castle. My stick is a sword. This kind of play often involves pretending to take on roles based on those we see around us such as parents, teachers, or hobgoblin war chiefs. This not only helps us formulate identities for ourselves, but it also lets us ease into the idea that minds other than our own exist. This is an empathy-inducing concept called "theory of mind" that we learned about in the last chapter.[2]

This play is natural, spontaneous, and frequently encouraged for children, but less so for adults. As we reach adolescence and our teenage years, the play we engage in becomes more structured and conforms to more socially acceptable activities. Sports. Competitive games. Maybe improv theater if you're hanging on tightly to the idea of pretend play. But at a certain point, your co-workers will not like it if you leap into the break room and shout "I'M A VELOCIRAPTOR! RAAAWR!" Ask me how I know this.

Fortunately for us, tabletop role-playing games have evolved into the kind of activity where pretend play is accepted. We're frequently encouraged to pretend, to some degree, that we're someone else, no matter our age or whether it's currently Halloween. And yet gaming groups vary in how *much* they encourage role-playing. This ranges from "barely at all" when players only want tactical combat on a gridded map, to "all in" when players want to lose themselves in role-playing and storytelling. A game's system of rules and rewards may drive role-playing—White Wolf's *Vampire: The Masquerade* or the *Fate* system by Evil Hat Productions emphasizes role-playing, for example—but that's only part of it. Other factors are likely at play within any given system that drive players to inhabit their characters. This then begs the question of what creates a group where role-playing is accepted and encouraged versus one where other players just smile politely and count the seconds until you're no longer enthusiastically pretending to be Speckles the halfling archdruid. In other words, what creates a culture that's supportive of role-playing where your alter ego of Speckles is welcome at the table? And what can you as a player or game master do to encourage role-play?

SETTING THE RIGHT GROUP CULTURE

Research in social psychology and psychology in the workplace may help answer these questions. One of the most important pieces of the answer can be found in the literature about organizational culture from the study of psychology in the workplace.[3] In one 2013 review of this topic, researchers defined **organizational culture** as "shared perceptions of and meaning attached to the policies, practices, and procedures employees experience and the behaviors they observe getting rewarded and that are supported and expected."[4] In other words, it's group members' understanding of what's smiled upon and what's frowned at. The concept can be fruitfully applied to any group, not just those in the workplace. That includes your gaming group. Any group's culture emerges over time through member interactions, but several things can have a big impact on culture formation.

First, rules and policies that promote the culture you want are probably the most important. In a workplace, examples of this include hiring processes, disciplinary procedures, and policies around work/life balance. The rules in a gaming group are unlikely to be this formal, but guidelines and expressions of player preferences are common. Recruiting potential players who are into role-playing is like hiring employees who support a culture of safety, customer service, or innovation. A "session zero" at the start of a *Dungeons & Dragons* campaign where everyone reviews house rules, themes, safety tools, and tone of the upcoming game is also a great place to say, "Role-playing is encouraged." And if the game master sets a policy of giving out bonus experience or inspiration points to players who role-play once things get started, that's a pretty strong parallel to reward and compensation systems that are key to reinforcing cultures in the workplace.

Second, research has shown that managers can have an outsized effect on culture in the workplace by modeling and rewarding desired behaviors.[5] Again, most gaming groups don't have such a hierarchical power structure, but we can take cues from the research nonetheless by noting that the game master is often seen as the game's "manager." Relative to players, they have a larger influence over the game's tone because they set house rules, control the game world, and hand out rewards. Most importantly, game masters can model the kinds of role-playing behaviors they want to see in others. They can role-play the haughty noble or the sanguine town priest. They also have more chances to role-play, since they have to give voice to every monster and non-player character in the game. Game masters can always find a way to role model a group culture friendly to role-playing.

Third, along with modeling the right behaviors, game masters and players need to communicate their desires and praise others when they role-play. Much like handing out bonuses or other rewards at work, simply telling a fellow player that you appreciate the in-character dialogue or deference given to character motivations will go a long way towards their repeating the behavior. So will telling the game master that you enjoy their coming up with voices for NPCs and giving them a bit of flavor.

In summary, here are some things you can do to promote a culture of role-playing in your group:

- Advertise that your group role-plays when seeking out new players.
- Do it yourself! People are less likely to be shy or unsure about role-playing if they see you do it.
- Express your desire for in-character dialogue and decision-making early on, preferably when the campaign kicks off.

- Reward those who role-play by giving them inspiration points, experience, or praise.

Once a strong culture for role-playing is created, a couple of other things can happen that open the door to more and better role-playing. One is what some researchers call **alibi**, which is when players begin to see the shared expectations for role-playing as their excuse for behaving as they do.[6] It's not me doing or saying these dramatic or funny things in an odd accent, it's the character. Why are you haranguing the NPC shopkeeper for high prices? Role-play! Why are you executing bandits instead of letting them live? Role-play! Why are you seducing the troll king? …Role-play? Leaning all the way into alibi can cause problems, though. Just because the group has created a social contract that role-play is expected doesn't mean the contract is a blank check for you to engage in inappropriate or intolerable behavior like stealing from your fellow player, attacking friendly non-player characters, using offensive language, or otherwise disrupting the game. You still have to read the room inside the game's magic circle.

 ## EMBODIED COGNITION

One of the most common ways players get into role-playing is to act out their characters' behaviors. Maybe the player gesticulates wildly during combat as they mimic swinging an axe. Perhaps they open their eyes wide in surprise or grimace in pain when they locate a hidden spike pit through the tried-and-true method of falling into it. And for the character actions that can't be captured in these small, accessible ways at the table, perhaps the player describes in vivid detail what their character does, such as grunting in satisfaction as their spear slips past an enemy's guard and pushes into its scaly hide. Game masters intent on bringing a great role-playing experience to the table also get into these kinds of antics by doing the same for non-player characters and monsters. Saying, "The ogre hits you for 14 damage" doesn't keep players in character as much as, "You take an involuntary step back and crane your neck up to see the bellowing ogre bring its club down on your shield arm, hitting you for 14 points of damage."

Why is that? Why does flailing around with our actual arms, mimicking emotions with our actual faces, and even imagining the actions and expressions of make-believe characters help us feel closer to what they are feeling, doing, and thinking? The cognitive psychology theory of **embodied cognition** responds to those questions and offers us some suggestions for how to role-play more effectively.

At the core of embodied cognition (also sometimes called "grounded cognition") is the idea that while the image of a living, thinking brain in a jar is very spooky, it's not very realistic. Brains live in bodies and they can't think about things without the benefit of all those body parts. "Thinking is for doing," as the saying goes. A bit more technically, our mental representations of things, even abstract concepts, are grounded in the brain's sensory systems for perception, movement, and awareness of our mental states related to attitudes and emotions.[7] These physical experiences stack up to form more abstract concepts and associated meanings that you can access when needed or prompted. Furthermore, a core concept in embodied cognition is that the same parts of our brains are involved whether we do something, see it done, or think about it being done. Whenever we think about something, we mentally *simulate* sensing it and performing whatever actions are associated with it. When you see a d20, or even just imagine one, the parts of your brain associated with rolling a die activate to some extent, maybe enough to activate your wrist muscles a bit. And moving your wrist like you were rolling a die can activate thoughts about not only rolling a die but also associated concepts like random chance or anticipation.

This is a key point that bears emphasis and unpacking. Thinking about an action simulates it in our brain, using systems related to perceptions, actions, attitudes, and emotions that we have associated with that action over time and through exposure to it. If you meet a very tall, menacing person you may spontaneously produce several responses related to these systems. You look up to see them (motor control), you feel apprehensive (emotion), and you notice their size and deep voice (sensory).[8] All of these responses are used for encoding knowledge in your brain about this big, scary person. Experiencing them again makes it easier for you to recall and make sense of that knowledge. You don't even have to experience those things again in the real world; thinking about them activates the same systems in the brain in similar ways.

As noted earlier with the "rolling a d20" example, research on this theory has also shown that activating motor systems that have become associated with a concept in this way can color our perception of what's going on in front of our eyes or in our imagination. In one experiment, people who were tricked into nodding their heads (ostensibly to test how well a set of headphones fit) responded more positively to a persuasive argument because they were making a head motion associated with agreement.[9] Another study forced subjects to approximate a smile by having them hold a pen in their teeth while reading *The Far Side* comics.[10] Such subjects reported the cartoons as funnier than did people not made to smile. People sitting in a warm room have been known to display more interpersonal warmth towards others[11] and carrying around a heavy clipboard can make you feel more self-important.[12]

WHAT GETS US TO ROLE-PLAY AND WHY SHOULD WE CARE?

This is why would-be role-players in *Dungeons & Dragons* should mimic their characters' facial expressions, nonverbal behaviors, and even larger bodily actions during the game. When taking your turn in combat, gesticulate with your own hands as you describe casting a spell or shooting your bow! Activating those parts of your brain by mimicking those actions will help you feel the things associated with them and bring you closer to feeling all the heroic, awesome things your character is seeing, feeling, or otherwise experiencing. Demonstrating the power of such simple gestures, one study had subjects watch classic *Loony Tunes* cartoons and then later try to describe to another person what happened in them. When physically prevented from using gestures, subjects had a harder time processing and describing exactly what Wile E. Coyote and the Road Runner had been up to.[13] So gesture away!

Facial expressions are also an important part of role-playing because they create empathy through the same mechanisms as big motions using your limbs. We recognize another person's emotions by mimicking their facial expressions or subtly activating the parts of our brain associated with this action, which allows us to mentally simulate feeling that emotion.[14] So if you want to sell what your character is going through when they're down to their last few hit points and staring down a charging owlbear, put on that expression of worry or panic. Not only for your benefit but for the benefit of your fellow players, too. Maybe you'll get more healing if the party cleric can empathize with you. It's worth a shot.

The point of all this is that because thinking about a concept, a person, or anything else activates systems related to motor activity, emotion, and perceptions, we have a powerful tool for role-playing by recreating those actions at the table, and by even describing them vividly. Game masters also need to remember this. Don't just say things like, "You fail your saving throw and take 5 damage from the trap." Describe what's happening to characters' bodies, what they're reflexive reactions are, and what their senses tell them. Players may not want a game master to dictate their characters' internal states like fear or apprehension, but grounded cognition theory suggests that it helps role-playing to describe involuntary physiological responses like "the hair on the back of your neck stands up" or "your heartbeat quickens" to help their role-play along.

Finally, grounded cognition is also an argument against metagaming if your goal is role-playing. When people take all these cues from their brain's various systems to simulate what's happening, the quality of that simulation will depend on how well they can ignore bits of information, sensations, or other parts of the simulation that are incongruent[15]—information that a player has but a character should lack, for example, or giving an abstract, rules-based explanation like, "the monster only takes half damage to slashing weapons," instead of saying something like, "You grunt in surprise as your sword meets unexpected resistance and leaves a slash only half as deep as you expected." The former introduces elements to the mental simulation that detract from the experience instead of enhancing it.

So there's a real case for flinging your arms around, raising your voice, and contorting your face for the sake of effective role-play, but a different psychological theory suggests the value of another role-playing tool: props!

ENCLOTHED COGNITION

Back in the early 2010s, a team of researchers led by Adam Hajo and Adam Galinsky from Northwestern University brought subjects into a laboratory and handed them one of two garments at random. Some of the participants got what the researchers described as a "medical doctor's coat." Others got "an artistic painter's coat."[16] Each participant donned their garment and performed a task requiring sustained focus and attention to detail, like looking at a pair of almost identical pictures and finding minute differences between them. The researchers were interested in whether wearing clothes associated with a profession requiring intelligence would make someone perform any better on the task relative to someone wearing clothes associated with a creative profession.

And it did! Those wearing a doctor's lab coat performed better on the attention-to-detail task than people wearing an artist's smock. The garment they wore led them to believe in themselves more and try harder, the researchers concluded. But that's not even the most interesting part of the study. What's amazing is that the doctor's lab jacket and the painter's smock were the same white, button-up coat. The only difference between the groups was what they were *told* they were wearing.

Hajo and Galinsky called this effect "enclothed cognition,"[17] and other research has replicated their findings. For example, another study showed that hockey players who wear black jerseys, a color often associated with villainy, were more likely to get into fights or garner penalties.[18] Much like how the theory of embodied cognition holds that physical experiences become inextricably linked to how we think about and imagine things associated with them, wearing clothes or possessing props triggers thoughts and meaning that have become associated with them. This can then affect our mental states and psychological processes. We may feel that we are smarter, more attractive, more talented, or more physically gifted—or the opposite of any of those things. Psychologists have written about how "clothes make the person" and how our appearance can affect how people think about us. Dressing appropriately for a job interview, for example, is wise because *looking* sharp makes it more likely that other people assume you *are* sharp. But Hajo and Galinsky's line of research is different in that it showed how wearing certain clothes can make *you* think you're sharp, too.

TTRPG players can try to make enclothed cognition work for them, like my friend I described at the top of this chapter who accessorized his bard character with a real-life electric guitar and wig. Or maybe you'd want to go with something more traditional like a lute, a lyre, or a bongo drum. You do you. But I'd wager that you don't have to go full cosplay to tap into the enclothed cognition effect. Simply holding a prop, placing an accessory, or donning part of a costume can help you get into your role-playing.

WHAT YOU LEARNED IN THIS CHAPTER

- A group's culture (which researchers tend to call "climate") is the shared understanding its members have about what things will be rewarded, punished, or expected.
- Group culture in support of role-playing can be achieved by communicating expectations, and rewarding role-play behavior and group members' modeling of that behavior, especially by game masters and others seen as "leaders" in the group.
- Embodied cognition (sometimes called "grounded cognition") refers to a family of theories that suggest our knowledge and cognition are grounded in the motor control, perception, and introspection systems of our brains such that those systems are activated whether we are thinking about something or actually sensing/doing/experiencing it.
- Enclothed cognition refers to the fact that the clothes we wear and the objects we possess can affect our state of mind and perception of ourselves.

HOW TO APPLY THIS CHAPTER TO YOUR GAME

- If you want people in your game to role-play, the game master probably has the biggest impact on creating a group culture for it.

- Make expectations about role-playing clear to new players who are considering joining the group.
- Whether you're a player or the game master, model role-playing for others by doing it yourself, especially early in the group's history.
- The game master should offer rewards and incentives for role-playing, even if it's just praise and appreciation.
- Move your own body to approximate what your character is doing and also be sure to imitate their facial expressions to take advantage of grounded cognition.
- If you can't do that, at least describe those actions and expressions as vividly as you can, both for your benefit and for that of the others at the table.
- Use props, costumes, and clothing to trigger enclothed cognition so that you leverage the symbolic meaning of those items and clothes.

CHAPTER 8
HOW DO PLAYERS JUDGE ALIGNMENT AND MORALITY?

My players and I don't always agree with me on the whole "good versus evil" thing. Sometimes I say, "Potato," and they say, "Put all the villagers to death." Take the tricky case of Venrick the vampire lord, for example. He was the central character in an adventure I came up with a few years ago. The player characters were sent to check in on a backwater village that the king had ignored and left unprotected for decades. Bandits had moved into the region and started doing what bandits do, which involved a lot of stabbing. Fortunately for the townsfolk, Venrick the vampire had grown tired of fleeing from ninth-level adventurers every time he took over an abandoned castle or mist-shrouded mansion. So he had shown up to the beleaguered village and offered the mayor what I thought was a fair deal: he would protect the village in exchange for some nonlethal bloodletting, the use of a spare crypt, and a modicum of gratitude. The people, in the way of fantasy townsfolk everywhere, once they decided not to fetch pitchforks and torches, leaned into the bargain and even competed for the prestige of being each week's honored blood donor.

Given the circumstances, it was a good arrangement for everyone involved, even if it needed to be kept a secret from the religious zealot of a king. Venrick got a low-key way to continue being a vampire and the gratitude of a bunch of mortals. The townspeople got protection and the freedom to generally continue their lives without any help from the king, who hadn't been offering it anyway. This arrangement was unusual because according to the *Monster Manual* rulebook, creatures like Venrick are always evil, self-centered, and bad news. But I liked this break from convention and was eager to see how my players would navigate a morally tricky situation. In my mind, the villagers thought they were doing nothing wrong, and I wanted to see how the players would react. Would they see Venrick as something other than evil, given his actions? Would they try to reason with him? Would they return and lie to their king, saying that they found nothing amiss in the village?

It turns out the players navigated this moral maze like a bugbear in a china shop. Then they set the shop on fire and made sure there were no witnesses to the arson. Specifically, upon figuring out the arrangement between the vampire lord and the town, the party's paladin struck down the town's mayor in broad daylight for "defiling yourself and siding with evil against your king." The rest of the party politely applauded as he did it. This set off a sequence of cursed dominos that ended with frantic persuasion skill checks on a mob of townsfolk who had decided to retrieve those pitchforks and torches after all, but for use against the player characters who were watching the sun go down knowing that the town's protector would be coming for them soon. Ultimately, the party escaped before dusk and reported back to the king, who sent troops to put most of the town to the sword just as the mayor had warned with his dying breath. This drove Venrick away and his absence allowed the bandits to come back and take over once the king's troops finished their executions and returned home. For the party's part in this, the now displaced vampire made it his afterlife's mission to harangue and accost them for the rest of the campaign.

I was honestly surprised by the party's choice to doom the village in this adventure and I was especially confused by the paladin's moral reasoning. It seemed that they had undone my tangled Gordian knot of moral choices by fire-balling it. I was tempted to have the paladin's deity send a burning bush that shouted "DUDE, WHAT?" before stripping away his holy powers for killing an unarmed and duly appointed town leader in cold blood. But the paladin's player seemed genuinely surprised at me in return. "Siding with a vampire is evil!" he said.

Was it?? This scenario and others like it are why I've come to hate the alignment system in *Dungeons & Dragons*. This approach to moral codes reduces all the potential complexity of every creature or player character down to a three-by-three grid with "chaotic vs. law-abiding" on one axis, "evil vs. good" on the other axis, and "neutral" options in the middle of each:

Chaotic Evil	Chaotic Neutral	Chaotic Good
Neutral Evil	True Neutral	Neutral Good
Lawful Evil	Lawful Neutral	Lawful Good

In theory, this allows for nine different cells on the grid, each with a unique moral code that determines how a creature or person will act once their alignment is situated on the chart. For example, ogres are listed in the *Monster Manual* as chaotic evil. They want to hurt others and serve themselves. Paladins are almost always good (often lawful good) according to the *Dungeons & Dragons Player's Handbook*.[1] They abide by mottos like, "If you're evil, you get the sword plus 2d8 radiant damage."

One problem with this approach is that most players can't agree on what the cells in the alignment chart mean. What's the difference, in practice, between Chaotic Neutral and Neutral Good? The description of a monster says it's lawful evil, but what does that mean when your party of adventurers comes rolling up on its lair and tries to kill it for no reason other than it exists? Even following the rulebook's gentle guidance that "for many thinking creatures, alignment is a moral choice,"[2] so that they get to sort themselves into their preferred alignment cell, the system neglects nuance. You could, following the letter of the game's rules, encounter a chaotic good vampire. A player could create a goblin character that's neutral good. However, the alignment system still doesn't offer much guidance when it comes to situations in which players and the other actors in our stories have complex thoughts, motivations, flaws, and desires.

This limits storytelling. Interesting stories usually involve moral ambiguity. "That creature needs to be defeated because it's lawful evil," or, "We should side with that NPC because she's neutral good," aren't very interesting moral decisions. If I'm your game master, I don't want to present black-and-white situations. I'm going to periodically splash the battle map with shades of grey and make you choose between actions that have multiple consequences, some of which will be bad for the other characters in the story. I learned how to spell "pyrrhic victory" just so I could give players paths that wind through the moral low ground. Not every time—sometimes it's sufficiently satisfying to put down hordes of zombies or push demons back into the abyss—but occasionally I want players to struggle to decide if their actions and those of the NPCs they encounter are *moral* or not without simply referring to their alignment. I like to have players think about how one character's moral code may be different from another character's. Or even have them explore how it's different from the code of the real-life player controlling them, which is where some *real* role-playing can emerge. And this isn't just for the game master's benefit. Players who engage with role-playing morality in a more sophisticated way can find it rewarding as well.

Wouldn't it be great if there were a better system for thinking about moral judgments, especially in the context of games? A system based on research by psychologists who have studied how people like you and me look at someone's behavior and decide if it's right or wrong, moral or immoral, good or bad?

Good news, everyone! There is such a system. Psychologists have studied the psychology of moral judgments for decades. They've looked at not only how people decide whether someone's actions are moral or not in a given situation, but also how they make those same kinds of moral judgments about characters in games. They've also examined how creators of those games can come up with situations, characters, and story beats that *shape* players' moral judgments so that they fret and debate over their decisions in a way that makes the story more meaningful and memorable. But you're going to have to leave your 3x3 alignment charts behind.

THE APPEAL OF ALIGNMENT INTUITIONS

One model that's useful for understanding how players think about morality is called **Moral Foundations Theory** (MFT). In 2001, a psychologist at the University of Virginia decided that research on moral beliefs frequently ignored the fact that people don't typically take a step back to think rationally and systematically about morality. Instead, we tend to form snap judgments called "moral intuitions."[3] These are strong, stable, and immediate moral beliefs that quickly arise whenever we want to decide if something is right or wrong. A few years later, researchers reported studies showing that there are a handful of cross-culturally relevant dimensions or concepts about which people tend to develop moral intuitions. What's more, their research suggested that different people have different sensitivities to these five moral markers. You can care a lot about a couple, a little about another one, and practically not at all about the other two. The five dimensions are:

- Care
- Fairness
- Loyalty
- Authority
- Purity

Replace good/evil and law/chaos with the items from this list and you'll have a good idea of how these ideas will relate to the game. Let's look at each of these in more detail before we get there, though. Maybe you can think of situations in which you've encountered moral quandaries as a player and in which some of these concepts came into play.

First, **Care** is what it sounds like: concern over the suffering of others, and having empathy for them. Its opposite is harm. Those who are particularly sensitive to Care violations are likely to strongly agree with statements like, "It can never be right to kill a human being."[4] People violating Care hurt other people while those upholding it minimize harm. A player's deciding whether or not to kill a bandit who surrenders when he realizes he's outnumbered would involve moral intuitions about Care. So would deciding that it was good that the vampire lord Venrick protected the villagers from bandit attacks.

Fairness is related to justice and reciprocation. It describes whether people get what they deserve and whether they play by the agreed-upon rules. People sensitive to Fairness are likely to agree with statements like, "I think it's morally wrong that rich children inherit a lot of money while poor children inherit nothing." Agreeing to follow through on a job the adventuring party was paid for involves fairness, as does splitting loot equitably among the party members. In my example from the top of this chapter, players focused on fairness might see the king's reneging on his obligation to protect his subjects as unfair.

Loyalty assumes a bias towards members of an ingroup (e.g., family or the adventuring party) and a bias against outgroup members (e.g., citizens of another nation or creatures from another plane of existence). The smaller or more tightly-knit the group, the more important it is. For example, loyalty to family is typically more important to moral judgments than loyalty to country. Upholding the precept of Loyalty in this way makes a person moral, but doing the opposite throws their moral standing off balance. Those sensitive to violations of Loyalty are likely to agree with statements like, "People should be loyal to their family members, even when they have done something wrong." A young wizard high in Loyalty, for example, is more likely to feel morally obligated to help her old mentor than to aid a stranger. A loyal soldier would see deserters from his country's army as detestable no matter their reason for leaving. In the case of the vampire and the villagers, players sensitive to Loyalty might approve of the mayor's decision to go behind his estranged king's back to broker the deal with Venrick, given that his townspeople, whom he swore to protect, wanted that outcome.

Authority deals with obedience to legitimate authority figures, such as the leaders of one's state, church, family, or guild. Obedience to these figures shows morality and opposition shows immorality, but this concept is not concerned with blind authority to illegitimate or irrelevant leaders. Those who place a lot of importance on Authority would be more likely to agree with statements like, "If I were a soldier and disagreed with my commanding officer's orders, I would obey anyway because that is my duty." In my adventure, obedience to the law of the land (by way of the king) would make exposing the villagers' deal with the vampire the most moral course of action.

Finally, **Purity** deals with keeping one's body and soul pure, unblemished, and free of contamination. Someone who abstains from drugs or alcohol might be seen as supporting this tenant of morality, while someone who eagerly replaces part of their natural body with cybernetic implants or magical orbs might violate it. Those sensitive to Purity would be more likely to endorse statements like, "I would call some acts wrong on the grounds that they are unnatural." In my example adventure, a character sensitive to Purity would feel that letting a vampire drink your blood is morally repugnant.

 ## MORAL SENSITIVITIES

Let's examine how people use these dimensions to make moral judgments. Moral Foundations Theory holds that when people see behaviors relevant to these dimensions, they form quick, intuitive judgments about whether they're being violated or upheld. Those judgments might even be unconscious. Of course, the bone devil is in the details here, and any situation or behavior can be interpreted differently vis-à-vis these principles. Will that dragon really be harmed if we steal just *some* of its treasure? Isn't this adorable goblin named "Skatz" a member of our in-group if we make him an honorary adventurer? Did the scheming noble house get more out of this trade deal than they deserved? Do we value preserving the druid's forest or side with the townsfolk who need wood for their buildings? Aren't dwarves *supposed* to drink excessively?

But that's the point of Moral Foundations Theory and the research that has gone into it. Different people have different sensitivities to each moral intuition.[5] Indeed, some recent research suggests that not only do we have differing sensitivities for these five moral intuitions, but they can also affect how we behave in role-playing games. In one study, researchers had 300 people fill out a questionnaire that measured how sensitive they were to each of the five moral intuitions of Care, Fairness, Loyalty, Authority, and Purity.[6] Armed with these baseline sensitivities to moral transgressions, the researchers then had participants play the computer game *Neverwinter Nights,* a role-playing game based on the *Dungeons & Dragons* license. The researchers had modified the game to present five scenarios (think side quests) that were each designed to deal with one of the five moral intuitions. In the Loyalty scenario, for example, the player character advised an NPC on whether or not to help out with the family business. The scenario on Authority involved orders from a local lord to take extreme measures to clear a magical blight. It's not hard to imagine tabletop *Dungeons & Dragons* players finding themselves in similar situations.

The researchers then recorded what decisions their subjects made in each scenario and compared them to which moral intuitions they were typically sensitive to. They found that when the game presented any of these five loaded situations, there was a significant relationship between a player's choice and their baseline sensitivity to the corresponding moral intuition. People sensitive to Care, for example, were more likely to resolve side quests consistent with that principle. Their out-of-game preferences drove in-game behavior. If the game designers, or game masters in the case of tabletop games, had information about the shape of players' moral compasses, they might select side quests and situations within the game to make them more interesting and morally charged.

MOVING MORAL FOUNDATIONS

Other researchers had this same idea of manipulating sensitivity to different moral dimensions and published a follow-up study a few years later.[7] They wondered: can the way a game *presents* and *frames* moral choices temporarily change people's sensitivity to these moral dimensions and thus coax them into leaning one way over another? This research used the same *Neverwinter Nights* scenarios as the previous study, and also first measured people's baseline sensitivity to Moral Foundation Theory's five moral dimensions. But then they used a device to very quickly flash in front of players certain words associated with upholding or violating moral principles. For example, the word "compassion" may have flickered across a subject's screen for 75 milliseconds to underscore the Care intuition. The idea was to prime players before each game scenario with words associated with the target moral intuition and thus temporarily make it more important when deciding how to have their player character react. While not ideal (it would be more compelling if the presentation of the scenarios themselves had been altered), the researchers point to their approach being successful in other contexts and a pretty reliable substitute.[8] Regardless, the researchers found that in some cases it was possible to use this technique to affect someone's moral choice in a video game, beyond what their baseline sensitivities were. They were able to sway some players' moral decision-making by getting them to think about certain moral intuitions before presenting them with a side quest where that value would come into a moral decision-making process.

Of course, most game masters won't flash subliminal messages at their players for 75 milliseconds before starting a game. You should be suspicious of the ones who do because they're up to something. But game masters *can* prime players in other ways. They can get them to think about Loyalty or Purity by having non-player characters talk about it or violate those principles before players are presented with a moral dilemma. They could drop in hints about what the party's patron values. They could discuss how a prophecy or curse was triggered by violating or upholding one of the moral principles. There are endless ways to bring these five dimensions up, but having the Moral Foundations Theory framework provides some structure around constructing moral quandaries and reacting to them as a player.

Indeed, if a player has mapped out her character's sensitivity to the five different kinds of moral intuitions, the game master could build situations, interactions, and choices around the ones that the character is most sensitive to. They could present a choice about Fairness knowing that the party's rogue is prone to extreme moral intuitions on this dimension, but the bard is not. That's potential for interesting role-playing and a much more interesting choice than deciding to do the "good" thing.

You could even imagine a homebrew moral intuition system integrated into character generation, where players have 15 "morality points" to spread across the five dimensions, up to a max of five in each.[9] A simple table to document these choices would suffice, but you could also use any spreadsheet program to create a chart like this to help guide that character's moral choices:

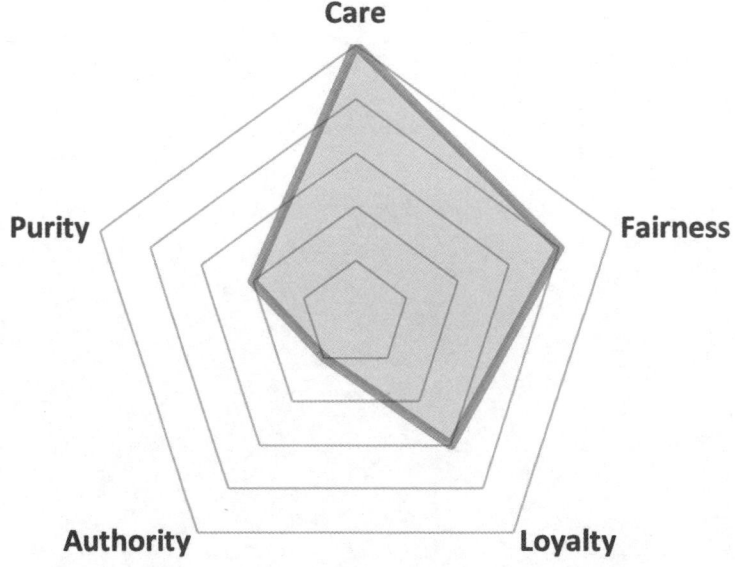

To me, this is a lot cooler than that 3x3 alignment table. Call it the "Pentagram of Morality" or the "Five-Sided Moral Compass." And it's backed by science! Even if you don't go this far, the next time you as a player encounter a moral quandary like a bunch of villagers befriending a vampire out of self-preservation, think about this Moral Foundations Theory model and ponder how your character would react given their sensitivities to different moral intuitions. Maybe you'd make the same decisions my players did because yours are maxed out on Authority and Purity. Or maybe you'd decide that your characters should keep the villagers' secret because you value Fairness and Care more.

 THINGS YOU LEARNED IN THIS CHAPTER

- Moral Foundations Theory offers a research-based alternative to good vs. evil and law vs. chaos when conceptualizing moral codes.
- It says that we decide if something is moral or immoral by forming quick, intuitive judgments about whether it upholds or violates five universal, cross-cultural dimensions of morality.
- Care has to do with caring about the welfare of others.
- Fairness has to do with reciprocation and getting what you deserve.
- Loyalty has to do with preferential treatment to those from your in-group.
- Authority has to do with upholding and obeying legitimate authority figures.
- Purity has to do with keeping oneself free from contamination.
- Research has shown that people have different sensitivities to these five moral dimensions and that they can temporarily be made more sensitive by drawing attention to them.
- Which all makes for a potentially interesting and fun way to think about—and test—your character's moral code.

HOW TO APPLY THIS TO YOUR GAME

- Use the five dimensions of Moral Foundation instead of (or in addition to) the good/evil and law/chaos alignment system from *Dungeons & Dragons*.
- Think about which of the five dimensions your character is most interested in upholding and which they care less about. This can still allow you to play a "good" character but with different priorities than your teammates.
- You could go so far as assigning points and creating the "Pentagram of Morality" described above to have a handy reference.
- To create even more interesting role-playing scenarios, create a character with sensitivities to different moral intuitions than you personally have.
- If you're a game master, create scenarios and role-playing encounters that might be resolved differently depending on which moral intuitions characters are sensitive to.
- Also if you're a game master, try priming players to consider their moral intuitions by drawing attention to specific dimensions through narration, NPC interactions, and lore.

CHAPTER 9
WHAT DO WE GET WRONG ABOUT UNLUCKY DICE AND NATURAL 20S?

The king of Norway once won possession of an island off the coast of Sweden by rolling a bunch of critical hits in a row, culminating in the equivalent of getting a natural 21 on a 20-sided die.

Back in 1015, the Viking mercenary-turned-monarch Olaf Haraldsson fought and talked his way to power in Norway, seeking to end the influence of foreign powers like the Danes and Swedes.[1] It was a tough job since many of Norway's Jarls were backed by those same powers, but Haraldsson eventually pulled it off and pronounced himself King Olaf II. Denmark was distracted by other problems, but Sweden continued to provide the new king with a steady supply of trouble. The King of Sweden—also named "Olaf," by some not-as-improbable-as-you-probably-think chance—blithely sent tax collectors into Norway and refused to accept that the country was under new management.

Skirmishes ensued, but both monarchs grew tired of the situation within a few years and decided to sit down and talk. The negotiations proceeded nicely until the two of them hit a sticking point: sovereignty over the aforementioned island of Hísing. Rather than having their soldiers resume hacking each other to death, King Olaf of Norway and King Olaf of Sweden agreed to a much more mundane solution: they would roll dice for it.

It was to be an Olaf roll-off.

The game was simple: each king would roll two six-sided dice—2d6 in tabletop game parlance—and the ruler who rolled the highest would win the island. The terms settled, the Swedish king started the show with a showstopper by rolling double sixes. We can all probably imagine the "Oooooh!" that went up around the table from personal experience. In this case, Swedish Olaf credited God for the luck, but the king from Norway grabbed the dice and put that in doubt by immediately rolling his own double sixes. Each monarch took turns rolling and every time the result was the same: twelve by way of two sixes. This went on until the dice were thrown so hard that one of them split in half. As silence fell around the table (or so I like to think) the spectators saw that the one, unbroken die still came up with a six. And so did half of the broken die, with its other half showing a one. Thus, the King of Norway won by rolling a "natural" 13 on 2d6.

To the extent that this story is true it must be because the dice were loaded, but the tale spread and remains interesting today because chance, especially strings of longshots like what the two Olafs experienced, is an important concept in games like *Dungeons & Dragons*. It's how we invoke randomness and make the game straddle that wonderful line between rules-driven board game and freeform storytelling. And it keeps things exciting: random outcomes are much more engaging and attention-getting than sure bets. We've all probably been in exhilarating situations where luck seems to be with us as we roll one success after another. Or maybe we've had one critical failure after another push us down the road to creating a new character after ours got plugged by too many arrows.

It's fascinating how we sometimes react to these flukes of probability and strings of harsh luck by trying to control or influence them. We invoke divinities. We ascribe agency and hatred to inert little pieces of plastic and put them in "dice jail" to serve time. We appeal to hidden rules of the universe that we ignored five minutes ago when things were going differently. And we willfully ignore logic and entire branches of mathematics because we feel like we should be *due* for a good roll.

Fortunately, psychology can not only help us understand this behavior but also curb it when needed. Researchers who study topics like gambling, risk assessment, consumer choice, and even sports fandom have found a long list of biases, fallacies, and misconceptions that people hold about randomness. Understanding those modes of thinking can help you understand what's going on between your ears and better embrace the uncertainty inherent to playing *Dungeons & Dragons*. Hopefully, you'll walk away with a better understanding of how randomness works, how the human mind tries to fool itself, and why you should not get so frustrated the next time you roll a two instead of a 20.

THE GAMBLER'S FALLACY

The first example of cognitive trickery around dice rolling has been invoked in many of the games I've played over the years. Imagine that your party is tracking down a necromancer. Suddenly, you are attacked by zombies! One of your fellow players rubs her hands together in anticipation. Her barbarian, she explains, will smash these zombies through the floor with her two-handed warhammer.

The player eagerly rolls when her turn comes up and gets a total of seven after all her bonuses, which the game master tells her is short of the eight needed to hit.

Undeterred, the player waits for her next turn and swings at the same zombie, which she describes as having a smug look on its face.

She gets a five.

Everybody at the table groans in sympathy, and on the player's next turn that zombie is not only still standing, but it has also been rolling much better and leaving bite marks on the barbarian's thick skull. Deep ones. So, another roll.

A six.

The player throws her hands up. At this point, one of the other players points out that his character is also pretty beat up and maybe now it's time to retreat or heal up. The barbarian's player, though, has other ideas. "Three misses in a row. I'm due for a hit, so watch this." She then announces that her barbarian will not only swing again but will use her "Great Weapon Master" ability that imposes a -5 penalty on her to-hit roll in exchange for a ridiculous bonus to damage if it connects. Because it *has* to connect this time.

She rolls a one, which with the -5 penalty drives her into negative numbers. The zombie, which thinks this whole series of events has been fantastic, eats what's left of the barbarian's brain.

Was this player right to think that she was "due" for a roll high enough to hit after three misses? The player here was falling prey to what psychologists call **the gambler's fallacy**. It's the belief that a successful outcome is guaranteed after a run of bad luck or failures. To put it in a slightly more technical way, it's ignoring the fact that independent events like die rolls have no effect on one another and that the result of each roll is assigned a fresh probability. Flip a coin, for example, and note the result. Whether it comes up heads or tails does not affect the outcome of the next flip. It's the same with rolling a d20: a 1 or a 20 or a 16 on one roll doesn't affect the probability of getting any particular result on the next roll.[2]

Unfortunately, our squishy human brains have trouble with this concept, especially when presented with a string of results that don't *look* purely random. One group of researchers asked people to describe 100 hypothetical coin tosses by typing out the heads or tails results with strings of Hs and Ts.[3] The hapless subjects were further instructed to talk out loud about everything that came to mind as they performed the task. These spoken streams of consciousness were collected and distilled by the researchers to identify the reasoning used for deciding whether the next result in the string should be an H or a T.

What they found were amazingly consistent flaws in logic and mathematical reasoning. Specifically, they found that:

1. People wanted their strings of results to have an equal number of heads and tails
2. They avoided long sequences of the same event such as H H H H H and would insert a tails result in there to avoid having too many heads in a row

A series of coin flips, most of these people muttered to themselves per the experimenter's instructions, was truly random only if all the possibilities happened equally across a small number of flips and if you didn't have too many heads or too many tails in a row.

But that's not true. Yes, if flips of a coin or rolls of a die are truly random you will get the same number of heads or sixes as you do any other result—but only over the very long run. In 100 coin flips, you may get 65 heads and 35 tails. It's quite possible. Roll a 20-sided die 100 times and you almost surely won't get *exactly* 50 rolls that are ten or less and 50 rolls above a ten. And you may get several results of one type or another in a row. This is what psychologists and other researchers often call **belief in the law of small numbers**: you expect a small sample of events to look just like the big, huge populations from which they're hypothetically plucked.

But they probably won't, and the smaller the sample the more likely the sequence will deviate from what you'd get in the long run. That's the rub with tabletop games like *Dungeons & Dragons*: we don't roll that many dice in the course of a combat, or an evening, or even a campaign. In one night of playing, we probably only make around a dozen rolls. Maybe two dozen if there's a lot of combat. You can have all low rolls. You can have a suspicious string of misses or even a string of critical hits. Like the subjects in the experiment I described above, you may think that's weird, but it will still probably happen occasionally. And sometimes we're completely, irrationally wrong about the randomness of dice rolls in yet a *different* way.

THE HOT HAND FALLACY

You as a *Dungeons & Dragons* player may have more in common with the 1981 starting lineup of the Philadelphia 76ers basketball team than you think. Imagine your wizard does what wizards do and casts fireball on a pack of rabid gnomes. Per the rules, the game master rolls saving throws for each of the five gnomes to see if it can avoid at least some of the fiery damage. That's going to be five rolls of a 20-sided die, and they have to roll, let's say 15 or higher. That's a 25% chance of success, from the gnomes' perspective. The first is a success. The second is a success. The third? Also a success. Wow, your game master is really on a hot streak, right? If a stern-looking man wearing a white lab coat and a name tag reading "EXPERIMENTER" were to ask you what you thought were the chances that the next die roll would also be a success, would your answer be greater than 25%? Probably, if you're honest and like most people. Would it be *less* than 25% if the game master had *missed* three rolls in a row instead of succeeded on them? You might think so. Put another way, have you ever seen someone on a hot streak with their dice rolls such that you expect them to do better than pure chance on their next roll?

A lot of people think they have. Some of them are very tall. In 1985, researchers Thomas Gilovich, Robert Vallone, and Amos Tversky published a watershed paper on what's called **the hot hand fallacy** with input from the Philadelphia 76ers instead of immolated gnomes.[4] They interviewed members of the basketball team during the 1980-1981 season about their beliefs in streaky shooting and hot hands. That is, do basketball players "catch fire" and make shots in streaks such that their success with a previous shot leads to greater chances of success on the next? Most of the players said that they "almost can't miss" a shot made after sinking a few buckets in a row. They believed that someone's chances of making a shot were as much as 13% higher when they were on a streak, which is huge when looking at success rates in basketball. What's more, streaks were thought to go in both directions. For free throws made by a person with a 70% base rate of success, the average chance of success was guessed to be 74% after making one shot and only 66% after missing one. This perception is important because it could drive whether a player decides to take a shot themselves or pass the ball to a player that they think is on a streak.

The researchers being researchers, however, wanted to look at the data. When they examined actual patterns of success and failure for the 76ers and other teams, they found no evidence of hot streaks. Players were not any more likely to make a shot after a series of successes, nor were they more likely to miss one after multiple misses. Of course, unlike rolling dice, basketball is a game of skill with many factors that could affect the success or failure of a shot: fatigue, the other team putting an extra defender on an opponent in the middle of a perceived hot streak, the player's willingness to take shots given their belief in streaks, among others.

But Gilovich and his colleagues factored these kinds of things into their analyses. This was especially true for their analysis of free throws, which involve fewer of these other variables and make it easy to compare success rates during streaks with a player's success rate over his whole career.

Furthermore, other research has found the Hot Hand Fallacy at work in pure games of chance, like those played in a casino.[5] Players often think that if they're on a roll, luck is with them, and the next roll, the next hand, or the next clatter of the roulette wheel will keep the pattern intact. It's the same with the game master making all those saving throws to help the gnomes. A lot of players will assume that the game master is on a hot streak that has nothing to do with fireballs, but they're forgetting (or ignoring) the fact that each roll is an independent event unaffected by the rolls that came before it no matter how unlikely the sequence looks.

MOTIVATED REASONING

At this point, the thoughtful reader (that's you) may be saying hey, wait a minute. If you look at a string of successful dice rolls, the Gambler's Fallacy and the Hot Hand Fallacy say different things about what the roller should think happens next. If you roll four successes, someone possessed by the Gambler's Fallacy should think that the next roll should be a failure because that many successes in a row doesn't seem random. But someone in the throes of the Hot Hand Fallacy would think that the pattern should continue because the roller is on a streak. And you're right. Both can't be true. But that's not the point: they're *both* wrong. They're both irrational and each results from a different misunderstanding of how chance works and how a random sequence should look when it's only a small sample of a much larger sequence.

Some research has found that we may shift from the wrongheaded thinking of the Gambler's Fallacy to the equally wrong Hot Hand Fallacy depending on what we *want* the next die roll to be and whether breaking the streak would be good or bad for us. One group of researchers had Portuguese basketball fans watch a game where the team they were rooting for went on a point-scoring streak. The experimenters then asked the participants if the streak would continue.[6] Most said yes. But when they watched a similar game where the *rival* team went on the same kind of streak, the same fans booed and claimed that the sequence of unanswered points was sure to break. Psychologists call this **motivated reasoning** because we're motivated to think in a certain way given our fandom, our optimism, or our undying hatred for the other team. Similarly, when it comes to *Dungeons & Dragons*, we tend to buy into hot streaks when such a belief makes us feel more optimistic or badass, and we stumble into the Gambler's Fallacy when we can't believe our bad luck or think the game master is out to get us.

In any case, you better cast another fireball. Those slightly singed gnomes look pretty angry. Although, what if the next die came up a 14 when you were hoping for a 15? Would you feel differently than if it came up as only a 2?

THE NEAR-MISS PHENOMENON

Slot machines used to be sneaky in a much more noticeable way. In what most of us think of as a traditional one-armed bandit design, players aim to get three symbols of the same kind to win. "Jackpot-Jackpot-Jackpot" means you win huge and might be able to buy a new boat or that miniature of a red dragon you'd been wanting. And given how the slot machine reels would snap into place from left to right, you can imagine widening your eyes upon seeing the first one land on Jackpot, clapping your hands as the next one did the same, and then holding your breath waiting to see where the third one hit.

And then seeing it stop on a cherry. Or a bell. Or some other worthless result that means you get nothing. NOTHING.

Except it doesn't quite feel like *nothing*. More often than not, missing by a hair is almost as exhilarating as winning the actual jackpot and people are more likely to plop in another coin and spin again relative to times when they got a losing result like "Lemon-Cherry-Bell." Because with "Jackpot-Jackpot-Cherry," they didn't *lose* per se. Instead, they *almost won,* which feels different. Slot machine manufacturers eventually noticed this and rigged their machines to have more Jackpot results on the first two reels and fewer on the last one so that gamblers would keep dropping money into the machines.[7] A similar trick was used during the 1970s for scratcher tickets where players scratch coatings off a card to hopefully reveal a winning combination.[8] This is the **Near Miss Phenomenon** at work: When we *almost* get the result we need from a die roll, we're more motivated to try again than we would be had we missed by a wider margin. Near misses activate the reward circuitry of our brains much in the same way that actual hits do, even though they *feel worse* and are *more frustrating* than wider misses.[9] But from our brain's perspective (which is the most important perspective, according to our brains), near misses are almost as useful as hits for making sense of the world and predicting how to get more of a good thing.

Maybe we're just wired this way, as many researchers think. Maybe the near miss creates frustration or regret in our minds that we're motivated to erase with a win on our next attempt.[10]

Whatever the reason, I see this come up in *Dungeons & Dragons* games all the time. Did you roll an 11 when you needed a 12 to beat that monster's armor class? You'll probably try the same attack next round instead of doing something different. So the next time you find yourself simultaneously excited and frustrated by a near miss, you can tell everyone at the table what the term is for that. Trust me, they'll be impressed.

DICE SUPERSTITIONS AND THE ILLUSION OF CONTROL

Sometimes, sociologists have the coolest jobs. Back in the 1960s, one such researcher named James Henslen spent weeks in St. Louis riding around with cab drivers and rolling dice with them during games of craps.[11] This counts as research for sociologists. Henslen noticed that the craps-playing cabbies consistently threw the dice with more physical force when they wanted a high number and more softly when they wanted a low number. They did this even though the force applied to the rolls doesn't matter; fair dice rolls are always random.

This is one of those things that once you know to look for it, you see it all the time in tabletop games. It's a dice-rolling ritual born of superstition. And be honest: you probably employ some ritual or account for some superstition when you roll dice. At least sometimes. Have you ever put your little plastic polyhedrons in "dice jail" so they can learn their lesson and roll better? Do you shake the dice in your hand a certain number of times before rolling them? Do you have one die for saving throws, another for attack rolls, and another for the dreaded death save? Does being the first person at the table to roll help put you higher in the initiative order? In my years of gaming, I've seen *all* of these rituals and beliefs espoused by fellow players, and myself at times. I'm a dice jailor. I have a little wooden box with "CURSED" scribbled on the side.

Why does this happen? One reason is how our brains react to random, unexpected events. Not the results of dice rolls in this case, but of the things that happen right *before* the rolls. Psychologists have long known that if you pair a reward with a desired behavior, animals and people are more likely to repeat that behavior. The psychologist B.F. Skinner famously did this with lab rats and pigeons when he rewarded them with food for pressing a lever or pecking a ball. Psychologists call this **operant conditioning**. Stimulus, behavior, reward, repeat.

Then Skinner did something a little bit wicked but a lot insightful. As described in-game researcher Nick Yee's book *The Proteus Paradox*,[12] Skinner set up a contraption that would dispense food at 15-second intervals no matter what the pigeons did. So the birds were just doing their bird things—bobbing their heads, waddling to-and-fro, looking up at the corner of the cage—when suddenly a tasty treat appeared! Because of how the birdbrains' bird brains were wired, the reward systems in their heads followed the same mental rut created by operant conditioning and assumed that whatever behavior they were doing when the food appeared had *caused* the food to appear. Skinner reported that many of his little winged subjects quickly seized on this and started repeating the behaviors all of them different behaviors—until the food appeared again 15 seconds later.[13]

In reality, the food was on a timer, but it's safe to say the birds didn't understand that. The coincidence was enough to cement a pigeon superstition. We're like those birds. Thinking that something happens because something else happened just before it can create those dice-rolling rituals and superstitions, even when randomness is to blame. Does it happen to everyone? No. Does the ritual sometimes peter out when it fails to work? Yes. But it takes surprisingly few pairings of ritual and result to lodge it in our mind, and the cost of following the ritual is often so sleight that we continue to do it anyway because what's the harm? Another psychological foible, **confirmation bias**, leads us to ignore or explain away the times it doesn't confirm our beliefs and remember the times it does.

Nick Yee provided another example of how this worked to create superstitions in the 2006 *Dungeons & Dragons Online* video game.[14] A bug in the game's code allowed players to use the Diplomacy skill on treasure chests containing random loot. Which, chests being intimate objects, makes no sense. Politely asking after the chest's family and avoiding delicate topics like lockpicks didn't actually do anything in the game. The bug just allowed you to make the pointless roll. Nonetheless, some lucky player must have done it at one time and found something spectacular after opening the chest, so the ritual spread. After the game developers got around to fixing the bug, players complained that the Diplomacy skill had been nerfed.

Another genesis of superstition and beliefs around dice-rolling relates to a tenacious psychological phenomenon known as **the illusion of control**. It has to do with people's tendency to think that they can exert control over chance events. It's part of a psychological immune system that inoculates us against the idea of our helplessness in the face of a cold, uncaring universe driven by random chance or forces too complex for us to understand much less influence.

Sorry, things got pretty heavy for a second there. The point is that we feel better if we think we have even a little bit of control over an event. So we're motivated to reason our way into that kind of thinking. Often this has to do with overblowing our perceived use of skill during events that we can directly influence (such as basketball free throws) but it also applies to the irrational attachment to superstitions and rituals.

This may also manifest itself in games of *Dungeons & Dragons* when we are given a choice to either roll dice ourselves or let the game master roll us. Do you let your game master roll for your character, or do you feel better about doing it yourself? This sometimes comes up when players want to make a Perception or Stealth skill check themselves. Seeing a low result like a two would let them know they surely failed, whereas more realistic suspense could be achieved if the game master rolls for the player and does not reveal the results. Most people still want to roll themselves, not just because rolling dice is fun but because it seems fairer, or like they've got better odds of success if they roll. As long as the game master isn't fudging results behind a screen, it shouldn't matter, but it feels like it does.

If you think like this, you're not alone. In one study, researchers increased people's illusion of control by having them remember a time when they were in charge of a situation or by telling them that they were going to be role-playing a manager dealing with a subordinate.[15] Others were told to remember a time when they had someone lording control over them or told they were going to be role-playing a subordinate dealing with their manager. Everyone was then told that they would win a cash prize if they predicted the result of a 1d6 roll. Furthermore, they were given the option of either rolling the die themselves or letting the experimenter roll it. The researchers found that those primed or instructed to think of themselves as in control tended to want to roll the dice themselves so that they could exert that control and win their reward. Whenever we grab the dice for ourselves, say a little mantra meant for luck, or pick the "good" die to roll something important, we're wrapping ourselves up in the illusion of control.

And maybe that's okay. Maybe it's less like we're wrapping ourselves in lies and more like snuggling into a warm safety blanket. It's nice to feel like you're in control. It's nice to be optimistic. It's nice to try harder because you think you're bound to succeed despite what some professor from the Department of Statistics might think. Playing *Dungeons & Dragons* should be fun and uplifting, even the parts that invoke (or seem to contradict) probabilities. King Olaf certainly thought so.

THINGS YOU LEARNED IN THIS CHAPTER

- The Gambler's Fallacy happens when we think that a relatively small run of die rolls can't continue because it wouldn't match what we view as a random result.
- The Hot Hand Fallacy happens when we think that someone is on a winning streak that is likely to continue. A similar error happens when we think a person is in a rut and missing all their roles, so they are likely to continue to miss.
- Both the Gambler's Fallacy and Hot Hand Fallacy lead to wrong predictions because they ignore the fact that each roll of the die is an independent event, unaffected by the rolls that came before it.
- Motivated reasoning is the term given to our desire to think ourselves into the Hot Hand Fallacy or the Gambler's Fallacy, depending on whether we want the pattern of rolls to continue or not.
- The Near Miss Phenomenon explains why it's so simultaneously frustrating and exciting to roll a 19 instead of a critical 20. Near misses activate the same reward mechanisms in our brains as direct hits.
- Good old operant conditioning helps explain why we believe in superstitions and rituals when it comes to rolling dice. Our brains mistakenly latch onto them as ways to predict the future much in the same way that we learn from real relationships between behaviors and rewards.
- The illusion of control is our tendency to think we can exert control over random or complex events. It's another driving force in adopting superstitions.

CHAPTER 10

HOW DO WE DEAL WITH SO MANY IN-GAME CHOICES?

Let's say you want to create a new character in *Dungeons & Dragons 5th Edition*. What species do you want to play? There are 15 to choose from in the *Player's Handbook* alone, including sub-types like rock gnomes and lightfoot halflings.[1] If you're using the expanded rules from *Mordenkainen Presents: Monsters of the Multiverse*, that bumps the number of species up to 49. Did you pick one that lets you have a feat to further customize your character? Nice, check out these six pages in the *Player's Handbook* covering the 42 options you have to pick from. Picking your character class is a simpler process with just 13 options, but there are a total of 117 sub-classes to choose from or plan for. Most classes have 8 or 9 subclasses, but if you're playing a wizard or cleric, you'll have to pick from between 13 and 14 subclasses, respectively. Then you'll need to pick one of 19 backgrounds, eight personality traits, six bonds, six ideals, and six flaws if you don't make that stuff up on your own. There are 18 skill proficiencies, 16 languages, and nine alignment options to consider. Oh, and you need to allocate points across six ability scores with an eye toward primary, secondary, and tertiary scores you'll want to emphasize. Done with all that and ready to spend your starting gold to gear up? Congrats, here are some tables with 13 kinds of armor, 38 types of weapons, seven types of packs, 37 types of tools, and 99 bits of miscellaneous equipment like candles, fishing tackle, and caltrops.

After all that you still haven't gotten to the open-ended choices about your character that you need to make. You have to pick a name, a gender, a height, a weight, skin/scale/fur/feather color, hair color (if applicable), and age. There are tables that let you roll for some of those qualities, but nobody leaves that stuff to the whims of the dice. Face it: you're going to rack your brain trying to come up with a good name and you'll be so mentally exhausted from making other choices that you'll just look at what's around you and shout "Fine! His name is Soda Can McCellphone! Can we PLAY already?"

Once you finally start playing, guess what? Playing *Dungeons & Dragons* involves MORE CHOICES. An infinite spool of choices will unwind before you as you explore environments, engage in combat, and interact with non-player characters. How do you try to get past the king's guards? Do you accept the woodcutter's quest to find his missing son or explore the abandoned fort? Do you shower the enemy goblins with magical fire or zonk them out with a Sleep spell? By design, the game presents you with never-ending choices.

And yet, most players would probably not want to give up all those options and wouldn't complain if you tossed in another set of optional rulebooks full of subclasses, species, feats, spells, and other character customization options. I talked in Chapter 2 about how important autonomy and meaningful choice are to games like this, but too many options can also be a problem. It can slow the game to a crawl, set players up for regret, and eat up mental resources needed for something else. Indeed, some research highlights the benefits of a "fewer choices is better" approach.[2]

 ## CHOOSING WITH DISADVANTAGE

In one famous study on choice, researchers Sheena Iyengar and Mark Lepper set up an experiment in the upscale Drager's

Grocery Store in Menlo Park, California. They had two stations staffed by research assistants posing as employees giving out free samples of "Wilkin and Sons" jam. At one station, shoppers got to choose from a parade of 24 different flavors. After an hour, the researchers put away that selection of jams and replaced it with a relatively paltry selection of just six flavors. They then rotated selections in this way for the rest of the day. Another researcher lurked nearby, keeping track of how many shoppers approached each version of the free sample table. Everyone who agreed to try a free sample was also given a $1 off coupon with a code that allowed the researchers to track which set of choices—the six-flavor or the 24-flavor array—resulted in more sales.[3]

The results of the study were clear: those who were presented with just six jam flavors to sample were more likely to pick one out and take it to the checkout lane. The weird thing is that more people stopped at the sample booth to take a look when they saw 24 flavors of jam on display. This mirrors my idea that *Dungeons & Dragons* players would say they prefer to be able to choose from a huge set of character creation options instead of a small set. What's amazing is that only 3% of people who perused 24 jam flavors bought something. But of the people who had to choose from just six flavors, over 30% bought a jar.

In the same paper, Iyengar and Lepper replicated this quirk of decision-making behavior in a different context involving Stanford University students who were given the option to write an extra credit essay about the 1957 movie, *Twelve Angry Men*. Half the students were given a list of six questions about the classic movie, one of which they were to choose and respond to in their essays. The rest of the students were given a much longer list of 30 essay prompts and asked to use one of them. As with the grocery shoppers sampling fancy jams, students who got to choose from a smaller list of essay prompts were more likely to do the extra credit assignment and their essays tended to be of higher quality.

In both the grocery store and the essay assignment studies, subjects found large numbers of choices more appealing but they were able to make up their minds more easily and were ultimately happier when they had a smaller number of meaningful choices. How should we apply this knowledge to TTRPGs? What effects do their unending barrages of choices have on players? How do games create choice architectures to make things more manageable? Once we make a choice, what determines if we experience regret later? Those are all good questions. Thankfully, we can explore answers in the rest of this chapter.

COMPENSATORY VS. NON-COMPENSATORY DECISION-MAKING

When people make decisions about things like vacation spots or starting character equipment, they generally adopt one of two approaches to choosing: compensatory or non-compensatory.[4] Both approaches involve a set of choices and a list of attributes to those choices that are important to the chooser. If you were buying a set of dice, your options are all the sets available in the store, and the attributes of those options might be the material the dice are made from, the legibility of the numbers, the colors, and the price. A **compensatory decision-making approach** considers the positive and negative attributes of ALL your options and allows for positive attributes to compensate for the negative ones or vice versa. But such an approach takes a lot of thought, effort, and information, so it's most often used when you have only a few options that differ in only a few ways. Otherwise, it gets overwhelming, fast. So a **non-compensatory decision-making strategy** is more likely to be employed when there are many options. Using this approach, one narrows down the number of options by eliminating alternatives that don't meet some minimum threshold for each desired attribute.

To make this clearer, let's look at in-depth examples of each approach in the context of TTRPGs. We'll start with something where a relatively simple, compensatory decision-making strategy would work. Many people play tabletop role-playing games online using virtual tabletop (VTT) software that simulates people sitting around a table. The number of VTTs on the market is growing, but it's still not huge. For the sake of illustration, let's say you're aware of Roll20, Fantasy Grounds, and Foundry. Since that's only three choices, you can compare your alternatives with a compensatory approach. Say you have this list of features that are important to you in a VTT:

- Price to get started with a homebrew campaign
- The extent to which it can automate tasks
- Stability of the software
- Ease of installation and updating
- Community support
- Ease of use for game masters
- Ease of use for players

You can do your research and score each of the three VTTs on each of these attributes using a simple 1 to 5 scale. This allows high scores on one factor to make up for low scores on another. For example, Fantasy Grounds is the most expensive of the options, but it does a great job automating things like tracking monster hit points when they take damage. So you tally up the points in each factor and go with the highest overall score. Easy!

Now let's look at a non-compensatory strategy more likely to be used when the number of choices is bewildering. Let's revisit the creation of a new character in *Dungeons & Dragons 5th Edition* as an example. Perhaps the first decision before us is choosing a class. Do you want to play an artificer, a barbarian, a bard, a cleric, a druid, a fighter, a monk, a paladin, a ranger, a rogue, a sorcerer, a warlock, or a wizard? That's a lot of options. Let's say you jotted down several important aspects on which to evaluate each option:

- Whether you have previously played the class before
- How many spellcasting options it has
- How well it will complement the overall party composition
- How fun you think the class will be
- Whether or not it fits the character concept you have in mind
- How powerful the class is in combat

Since there are 13 class options, scoring each one of them and comparing them systematically is too cumbersome and time-consuming. Instead, you would probably adopt a non-compensatory approach where brain power is spent not on figuring out the important aspects of each subclass compensate for each other, but on how they can be used to eliminate classes that don't meet minimum standards for each feature. Following this approach, you start with the aspect most important to you, eliminate options that don't meet that standard, then move on to the second most important aspect, and so on. This is called **elimination by aspects**.[5] Let's assume that the bulleted list of factors above is sorted in order of importance. So you may first decide to eliminate the bard, paladin, and monk classes from your list of options since you played those in previous campaigns. Next, you may decide that spellcasting is fun so you eliminate any options that aren't full casters with spell lists that go all the way to level nine. So everything left that's not a druid, sorcerer, or wizard gets stricken from the list of remaining options. And so on until you are left with just one choice. Or if you can't get to one choice, you may add additional aspects by which to keep whittling the list down or even switch to a compensatory decision strategy once the list of options is small enough.

TRAPS, PROBLEMS, AND PITFALLS

On the face of it, the elimination by aspects approach lets you make sure that you have arrived at the best decision, whether you dove into that mode of thinking thanks to a small set of options or you arrived there by narrowing down options based on a non-compensatory approach. It seems rational. Data driven. However, you still have to look out for potential pitfalls. One is known as **the distinction bias.** It happens when we overestimate how much the difference between two options will impact our satisfaction when we consider them at the same time versus individually. For example: would I like a chocolate donut? Yes, I think I would be very happy to have a chocolate donut because chocolate donuts are delicious. Follow-up question: would I rather have a cinnamon donut OR a chocolate donut? Which outcome would be better? One of them has to be better, right? Well, I enjoy the smell of cinnamon more than the smell of chocolate, so maybe chocolate donuts aren't as awesome as I thought. You can see how my evaluation of a chocolate donut dropped when I had to come up with a trait (smell) with which to compare it against other options. Then I overweighed the importance of smell. The two treats considered simultaneously, the cinnamon donut came out on top, but I might have been equally happy with the chocolate if that had been my only choice.

Researchers from the University of Chicago demonstrated how the distinction bias worked in one study by asking subjects to imagine that they had published a book.[6] Some of the subjects were asked to make three simultaneous ratings: one each for how happy they would be if the book sold 80, 160, or 240 copies. Call them group A. Different people in group B were asked to make just one rating for how happy they would be if their book sold 80 copies. The other sales figures weren't mentioned to this group. Similarly, group C was asked to make one rating based on 160 copies sold, and group D was asked to do the same for 240 copies. The researchers found evidence for the distinction bias: when subjects in group A considered all three sales outcomes simultaneously, they predicted they would be significantly happier in the 240-copies sold scenario than in the 160-copies scenario, and significantly happier in the 160-copies scenario than the 80 copies one. But this was wrong from the perspective of the people in groups B, C, and D who were asked to just consider the one sliver of the multiverse in which they sold 80, 160, or 240 copies respectively. Comparing those groups' expected happiness revealed that they would all be roughly equally happy. Just selling 80 copies would be great! It was only when considering the possibilities of selling 160 or 240 copies that people became less happy with 80. Nobody could look at all three options simultaneously and say, "Oh, I'd be happy with any of these." We feel compelled to think that differences between options must matter, sometimes a lot. This suggests that you should just play one of the *Dungeons & Dragons* classes that meet your basic criteria and get on with it; you'll be equally happy in any case.

Maybe keep your reasons to yourself, though, because other research has shown that we can also run into problems when we are **asked to explain our decisions**. When this happens, we tend to focus on the most salient or plausible explanations and then give them a lot of weight.[7] One study, for example, sat people down in front of five posters.[8] Two of the posters were prints of widely celebrated art: Claude Monet's *Water Lilies* and Vincent van Gogh's *Irises*. The other three paintings were less likely to be featured in an art history class. They featured cartoon cats with humorous captions. Across both groups, half of the subjects were given a questionnaire asking them to rate how much they liked each of the five posters. The other half were also asked this but were then required to write down the reasons for their ratings. This created two main differences between the groups. First, when invited to take home a copy of any single poster they wanted, subjects who had to explain their ratings were more likely to pick a funny cat poster instead of fine art. Additionally, those who took home cat posters were less happy with their choice when the experimenters followed up with them weeks later and were less likely to have hung it up in their room. The authors argue that a layperson may have trouble explaining the appeal of something beautiful but abstract like a Monet or van Gogh painting, but they can much more easily come up with reasons to like a poster featuring a cat dangling from a rope and the caption "Hang in there!" Those who gave no explanation were free to go with the strong but ineffable impression that the fine art made on them.

To return to the "choose a character class" example from earlier, if you were asked to explain why you included "spellcasting options" as a criterion, you might feel compelled to take away points for the warlock because they're not as flexible as clerics or as good at dealing out damage as wizards. This might lead you to ignore other aspects of warlock spellcasting and the delectable flavor they bring to roleplaying and utility. This is similar to another concept that psychologists call **lay rationalism**, our tendency to overvalue attributes that have an obvious, quantifiable value (like doing 6d6 fire damage) and downplay anything that seems subjective (like having fun). Your decision-making process and reaching for accompanying explanations that sound plausible could lead you to reject a potentially better choice.

MAXIMIZING OR BEING SATISFIED

During one *Dungeons & Dragons* adventure I ran, my players encountered an odd fellow hiding away in a remote cave. The old codger offered to spin gold coins into a magical item for each character. I told the players that this was a chance for them to get some new loot and that they could pick any common or uncommon magic item they wanted from the rulebook.

This was a mistake. It brought the game to a complete halt. I'll never do it again.

Why? Because the players had over 200 magic items to choose from. And while a couple of the players quickly identified something that sounded good to them, others simply could not make up their minds. This little decision-making bomb I threw into the middle of my own game illustrates what researchers studying the psychology of choice call **satisficing** and **maximizing**.[9] Satisficing means you stop looking once you come up with a good option. Note that this doesn't mean that you make substandard choices; you still have minimum requirements for an acceptable option. Satisficing just means that you'll be satisfied with something good even if you're not sure it's the *best*. The player in my group who said, "Gimme a +1 sword, that sounds good" satisficed. Was there a better choice? Maybe, but a +1 sword is a nice upgrade so let's go.

Maximizing, on the other hand, means you exhaustively research every option for a decision and pick the one that's the *best*. The best option is the one that provides the most value, satisfaction, or whatever you're using to define a good choice. Maximizers can't stop looking after seeing that +1 sword on the list of possibilities. They have to put a pin in it and keep searching in case there's something *better*. Some boots that let their wearer walk up walls could be great in certain situations, but wouldn't a cloak that boosts armor class deliver more consistent value? Oh! What about a wand that shoots magic missiles? A couple of my players went on like this for almost an hour while the rest of us tried to get on with the adventure. They looked up different magic items, read their descriptions, and compared their merits. One of them even wanted to sleep on it and get back to me at the next session. I would have better served the game by offering a shorter, predetermined list of magic items for them to choose from instead of the entire universe of such items.

Does maximizing result in better decisions? There's some research showing that it does, and it makes sense that all that extra effort would pay off. But some of that same research suggests that maximizers may be less happy with their optimal choices in the long run. One study looked at college graduates entering the job market and identified the habitual maximizers and satisficers among them.[10] The maximizers ended up with salary offers that were, on average, 20% higher than their satisficing peers. That said, the maximizers reported feeling more stressed, anxious, overwhelmed, and unhappy during the job search. They also reported being less satisfied with the job offer they eventually accepted.

TAKEBACKS OR NO TAKEBACKS

Something else that can affect our satisfaction with a choice is whether or not we can take back the decision and choose differently if we decide we don't like it. Only it doesn't work like you're probably thinking. Because while most people would probably relish a guarantee that lets them undo a choice in favor of something else, this flexibility may make us *less* satisfied. You may end up happier if you know there are no takebacks.

One group of researchers cornered students in a photography class and had them shoot a bunch of photos with 35-mm cameras using old-school film.[11] Toward the end of the course, students were taught how to develop the film prints in a darkroom and were asked to pick their two favorite snapshots. A researcher then told the students that they could keep one of the prints as a souvenir while the other would be put on a boat and shipped overseas. For half the students, the researcher added that the print wouldn't be sent off for another five days and that the students could swap the prints if they changed their minds. For the other students, no such grace period was offered and their choice was irrevocable.

Nine days later, the researchers leaped out of bushes (I like to think) and asked the startled students how happy they were with the picture they had chosen to walk away with. Those who hadn't been allowed to change their minds said they liked their photos significantly more than those who had the option to walk back their choice. Why? Because we humans are adept at talking ourselves into feeling good about our current situation. Not always, mind you, but often. Regret is a real experience for everyone at one point or another, but for little things, we're good at not only seeing the silver lining but ignoring the cloud altogether. As the authors of the photography study state, "Human beings are famous for seeking, attending to, interpreting, and remembering information in ways that allow them to feel satisfied with themselves and their lot."[12]

This has been called many things in the psychology literature: positive illusion, self-deception, ego defense, dissonance reduction, emotion-based coping, self-serving attribution, dissonance reduction, and subjective optimization. They all amount to similar enough concepts for our purposes here. Think of it as a psychological immune system that shelters our egos when our choices turn out to be suboptimal. This helps us take risks and live with the consequences by changing what we can: our attitudes and cognitions about how things turned out. If we can change our choices we do so, but if not, we can often easily change our attitudes instead.

None of this is to say that players shouldn't be able to roll up a new character if they discover that they're not having fun with the one they've built. Or exit a group that they're not enjoying being a part of. But if you're a game master, think twice before you let players undo less consequential cursed choices. Because if they have to live with it, they might learn to love it.

WHAT YOU LEARNED IN THIS CHAPTER

- Modern versions of *Dungeons & Dragons* (and many similar TTRPGs) demand a lot of choices.
- In the face of a huge number of options, people may decide not to choose if they can, but if they have to, they may end up less satisfied than if they had fewer options.
- A compensatory approach to choice means that we evaluate all options against a set of features and then add up the scores, allowing a strong standing on one feature to compensate for poor showings on another.
- A non-compensatory strategy involves rank-ordering the features of options according to what's most important to us and then eliminating options that don't meet each feature's minimum threshold.
- We typically employ compensatory strategies when we have few options and non-compensatory in the face of many options.
- The distinction bias describes how we often overestimate how much the difference between two options will impact our satisfaction; it happens when we consider options jointly, but not when we consider them individually.
- Being forced to explain the reasons for our choices may lead us to overemphasize features that are quantifiable, easy to explain, and more socially acceptable.
- Satisficing is an approach to choosing where you take the first option that meets your standards for a good choice while maximizing involves continuing to search for better and better options until you identify the best one.

- We usually value the ability to change our minds if we later decide we want to, but having to live with your choice may motivate you to talk yourself into being happier with it.

HOW TO APPLY THIS CHAPTER TO YOUR GAME

- If you are a game master, create choice architectures for your players that make sense and that ease the burden of considering so many choices. Examples include offering pre-generated characters to first-time players, dividing classes up into archetypes like tanks, strikers, healers, etc., and giving them a limited list of magic items to choose from.
- If you're a player, make use of those tools that the game offers to simplify itself. Take the pregen. Start the character creation process by looking at archetypes and then sticking to one. Don't complicate your life with optional rules like multiclassing or feats. Get in. Get going. Live with your choices.
- If those choice architectures aren't present or don't help, find ways to use non-compensatory decision-making and rules of thumb to get to a manageable number of choices that you can handle more comprehensively.
- If you are a player, don't feel like you have to justify your actions; a good game master will find ways to make any choices you make fun and rewarding. Likewise, don't try to argue with other players about whether what they're doing is optimal.

- Speaking of optimal, don't be a maximizer unless you can do it without disrupting the flow of the game. You're not choosing a career, deciding where to go to college, or making any life-altering decision with high stakes. Take the +1 sword and get on with having fun. If you absolutely must consult every bit of information you can find, do it away from the table.

PART III
PARTY DYNAMICS

CHAPTER 11
WHEN DO PLAYERS WORK TOGETHER BEST?

"Okay, what do you all want to do?"

If you've played *Dungeons & Dragons* or any other TTRPG, you've been confronted by this question. Repeatedly. Sometimes it's explicitly asked, sometimes it's implied by statements like, "It's your turn." It's largely why you're at the table instead of watching a movie, reading a book, or playing a video game. TTRPGs are freeform because a call-and-response mechanic lies at their core. First, a player decides what they want to do and announces it to the game master. Second, the game master decides what happens. If what the player wants is covered by the game's rules, the game master adjudicates those rules, and dice are used to invoke randomness as needed. Finally, to close the loop, the game master reports back on what happened as a result of the player's action.

This call-and-response approach creates a flexible and open-ended system that, when it was first implemented by the creators of *Dungeons & Dragons* back in the 1970s, was shockingly different than most wargaming and board game systems. As Jon Peterson notes in his detailed history of role-playing games *The Elusive Shift*, "Anything the referee can describe verbally can become an element of the game, and anything a player can articulate as a statement of intention can potentially translate into an action."[1] This puts control not only in the hands of the game master but also shares it with players. Players need to exercise choice and shape the story for themselves, but then they need to work with other players to do the same for the group. This often means coordinating different abilities, preferences, and rules that aren't relevant to all players at once. It can also involve much more elaborate plans like collectively deciding how the story should unfold and how to structure its major beats. In this chapter, we'll look at situations in which players need to employ teamwork, starting with using knowledge about other party members to coordinate.

UNDERSTANDING YOUR PARTY

My friend Allen had a problem. Given that our party was plumbing dark, icy caves and skulking around in the perpetual twilight in the frozen north, his choice of the Gloom Stalker subclass for his ranger seemed solid. Mostly because, as the name implies, the Gloom Stalker stalks in the gloom or, even better, in complete darkness. In the dark, Allen's character could not only see perfectly well but he was invisible even to creatures that could also see in the dark. This activated several powerful mechanics in the game, like making him harder to hit and making it easier for him to hit others for lots of damage.

The only problem was that some of the other party members couldn't see squat in the dark. Our aarakocra wizard and our fairy fighter would be blind. So we discussed, strategized, and made a plan to acquire Goggles of the Night (night vision goggles) for the fairy and the "Darkvision" spell for the aarakocra. To top it off, we added spells to the party's repertoire that would allow us to extinguish light sources so we could all scream, "I AM THE NIGHT!" as we stabbed monsters to death with impunity. It worked well and several combat encounters and bits of exploration were made much easier and more entertaining.

WHEN DO PLAYERS WORK TOGETHER BEST?

A psychologist watching us might recognize what we did as making use of **shared mental models**. The concept was first used by cognitive psychologists to describe a person's understanding of a system such that they could predict what will happen within that system.[2] You have a mental model for a car, for example, or a football game. You know the pieces at play, you know how they interact, and if you know the states of various parts of the system you can predict what will happen within it, and thus be ready to run with it or to stop it. Or to scream and run away. Researchers interested in high-performance teams have expanded this concept to *shared* mental models that team members have about their team and its tasks. The idea is that each member develops and maintains a complex mental model of the group, including what work was expected of it, the tools and technology involved, the capabilities and status of each team member, and how each member was impacted by the activity of the others.[3] Team members with accurate, overlapping mental models can coordinate and synchronize their work towards shared goals because they can leverage that understanding of what everyone else is responsible for, capable of, and aware of. Everyone knows that Dana the computer programmer can code in Python and Dizzwin the druid can shape-shift into a python. And that both of them are proficient in the Deception skill.

Research has reinforced the link between accurate, shared mental models and team performance, especially in high-pressure cases where members don't have the luxury of time to extensively communicate. One study found that leveraging shared mental models helped crews at a nuclear power plant respond more quickly and effectively to a mechanical malfunction that could endanger thousands of innocent people.[4] Other researchers had teams of subjects play the flight simulator game *Falcon 3.0* and measured how much overlap there was between members' mental models of what everyone needed to do.[5] They found that the more complete members' mental models were and the more overlap there was in the mental models of team members, the better the teams were at piloting and landing virtual fighter jets. This theme runs through the body of research on the topic: accurate, shared team models allow each member to perform better and help the team succeed.

Are *Dungeons & Dragons* parties the same as work teams? No, not exactly. Teams in a workplace admittedly have constraints and outside pressures that don't exist in games aimed at having a good time and making players feel powerful. They have to deal with market competition, budget allocations, and labor constraints, for example. Furthermore, the events in a *Dungeons & Dragons* session hardly unfold in real time. It's a game where a day-long trek across the wilderness can take six seconds of real time but a six-second combat round can take an hour. Conditions where real-world teams lean on shared mental models to minimize the need for communicating and strategizing during power plant failures or fighter jet combat aren't the same as tabletop games where players can take the time to talk and plan out everyone's combat actions ad nauseam. That said, party members' roles are enough like jobs and player characters are enough like teammates to allow us to use this research to understand how players can be more effective, especially when considering the combat and exploration pillars of the game.

For example, researchers have identified two broad types of team mental models that can be shared among team members: task mental models and team mental models.[6] **Task mental models** relate to the things the team hopes to accomplish and the equipment or technology that they can use to do it. In a *Dungeons & Dragons* game, this would include an understanding of the team's objectives both on a near-term basis (survive an attack by giant spiders, then navigate a rickety rope bridge) and long-term (solve the mystery of the king's disappearance and save the kingdom). Research on task mental models also includes an examination of the technology and tools teams use, so in the context of a game, it would include everything that player characters have at their disposal to accomplish their tasks—not only items, weapons, and equipment, but also spells, class abilities, and even game mechanics. If a player uses a class ability to trip an opponent knowing that another player's rogue can add sneak attack damage on his next hit because the target is lying on the ground, then those two players are using a shared mental model about their characters' abilities and the game's mechanics. If a player character who specializes in defensive fighting stands next to the party cleric and intercepts blows, they are using a shared mental model about the mechanics of breaking concentration and maintaining spells. Likewise, players that temporarily ignore zombies that are affected by a cleric's Turn Undead ability are sharing a mental model about how that ability works, knowing that damaging those zombies would make them hostile again. Could players compensate for poor mental models by talking to each other across the table and explaining all this? Yes. Do we frequently do that? Undoubtedly. But players make fewer mistakes and get through combat faster when they have shared mental models.

The second broad category of mental models is **team mental models**. These cover team members' understanding of player roles and expected behaviors, plus their knowledge of what every other member is capable of doing. If you're playing a cleric, a high-functioning team will implicitly share the understanding that you're supposed to undo damage, while the barbarian will be expected to soak up damage, and the wizard will need to dish out damage. This knowledge extends to knowing statistics about other characters, such as armor class, movement speed, skill check modifiers, saving throw proficiencies, resistances, and a dozen other things.

The player of a gruff cleric who defers to another player's eloquent bard when the party needs to convince a warlord to release prisoners is sharing a mental model about how the bard has a higher bonus to her Persuasion skill. Sharing team mental models also means that players track the state of characters besides their own. How many hit points do they have? How many spell slots have they used? Potions quaffed? Limited use abilities spent? Are any party members poisoned, exhausted, prone, blinded, invisible, restrained, or charmed? To the extent that players have and share these models, the better they perform and the more efficiently they take their turns.

That said, it's worth noting that, "I'm using good shared mental models!" is not an excuse for **metagaming**, which is a term for having a *character* act on something that only their *player* knows. For example, a player is metagaming if their fighter switches to a war hammer after reading in the *Monster Manual* that skeletons are vulnerable to bludgeoning damage. If the character had come upon this knowledge through in-game experience or the wisdom of a grizzled undead hunter they shared an ale with the night before, that's one thing, but players should always be aware of the difference between *their* mental models and the models their *characters* would have had a chance to develop. This also applies when a player knows that their teammate's *character* in another part of the dungeon needs rescue because the other *player* is sitting right next to them. It's hard to remember to switch between these different mental models while playing, but it's in the spirit of the game to do so. Recall the discussion of three different frames of experiencing a game from Chapter 6: real world, character, and game rules. Players can view the game through these three lenses and keep in mind that their mental models should differ across each of them.

WHEN DO PLAYERS WORK TOGETHER BEST?

So how does a group develop better shared mental models? Mainly, they will grow and overlap through experience and play, just as they do with any team. The more familiar you are with the rules that govern your character, the richer and more complete a mental model you will create. If you play different kinds of characters across different campaigns, that will help. That's the first piece of advice: play different classes across different campaigns. A second piece of advice would be to play other people's characters. If their owner and the game master are okay with it, you can play someone's character in addition to your own if that person is unable to make a given game session. If you can't do that, at least read through the rules on their class, the spells they have selected, and the magic items they own. You can accomplish something similar by playing friendly non-player characters, sidekicks, and henchmen that the game master normally controls. Finally, have after-action reports with your fellow party members where you discuss what happened in the previous session. Talk about how you could have synergized better, prepared more effectively, and shared ideas. You can even role-play it like your characters are sitting around the campfire if you want to avoid meta-gaming. Just make sure you share information so you can find and fill the gaps in each other's mental models.

"I CAST BRAIN STORM"

Critical Role is a popular show where professional *Dungeons & Dragons* players stream themselves to the internet for anyone to watch. During one episode entitled "In the Belly of the Beast," (spoilers in the remainder of this paragraph) the party had to slap together a plan to defeat an ancient black dragon due to descend on them the next day.[7] The players rose to the challenge by throwing out ideas and having their characters role-play their implementation. The mechanically inclined Percy went to work constructing a trap to pin the dragon to the ground. Keyleth the druid implored the village leaders to help in the fight and offered to use her magic to dig a trench from which they can launch an ambush. Other members started swapping armor and weapons that would give them an advantage against an acid-spewing dragon. The rogue Vax and the impish bard Scanlan came up with the most outside-the-box idea of all: to teleport up the dragon's cloacae (google it if you dare) and into its stomach, where they could pin it down with an Immovable Rod—a magic item that does what it says right there in the name.

As an example of brainstorming in *Dungeons & Dragons* games, this episode of *Critical Role* is iconic. Maybe you've never come up with an idea that involved a dragon cloacae, but if you're a TTRPG player, your game master has probably asked, "Well, how do you all want to approach this?" Maybe you need to navigate the frozen floes of a river. Maybe rescue the innkeeper's bratty son from a goblin cave or extract a bejeweled tooth from a statue surrounded by frothing-at-the-mouth cultists. For that last one, do you send the rogue to sneak in and pluck the jewel unnoticed, or create a distraction to entice the cultists to leave the room? Or do you use magic to disguise the bard as the elder god the cultists were trying to summon and demand that they fork over the treasure?

What are the cognitive mechanisms in play when we brainstorm and what can social psychology tell us about how we share our ideas and react to the ideas of others? Research in this area started way back in 1957 with the publication of a book called *Applied Imagination* by advertising executive Alex F. Osborn.[8] The "F." stood for his middle name of "Faickney" which isn't relevant here but I mention it because I think it's super fun to say. Try it.

Osborn famously coined the term "brainstorming" and formulated four rules for groups trying to pump out ideas. To paraphrase:
1. Don't criticize anyone's ideas, including your own.
2. No idea is too zany! Say everything that comes to mind, even the wild stuff.
3. Focus on quantity of ideas, not quality. Get as many ideas out there as you can.
4. Combine ideas wherever possible to come up with improvements.

Osborn insisted that following these rules would allow groups to outperform an equal number of individuals sitting in private and coming up with their own ideas.

Only he was pretty much immediately proven wrong, empirically. What a twist! Yes, it was true that these instructions let a group perform better brainstorming relative to a group that received no such instructions. But in 1958 a group of researchers showed that the collective efforts of people individually jotting down ideas on their own and then coming together to share tended to produce not only more ideas, but better ones.[9] Unfortunately, the things that cause brain storms to turn into a drizzle are likely to afflict most groups of *Dungeons & Dragons* players.

The first factor that hurts party brainstorming is **evaluation apprehension**. This is when we self-censor ourselves for fear of being judged by others.[10] Should I suggest that my character try a diplomatic solution with the Ricktus Finkus, Almighty Rat King of the Undersewer? He seems reasonable for a rat king. But no, I can think of several reasons why this wouldn't work, and everyone else seems to have their hearts set on violence. I don't want to come across as soft on rat kings or as one of those people who wants to hog the spotlight. Instructions for brainstormers not to criticize any ideas are designed to counteract this tendency to self-censor, but research has found evaluation apprehension a difficult trap to disarm.[11] Other research has found that when people complete brainstorming with electronic tools in ways that make them feel anonymous, they tend to perform better than in groups where the owners of ideas are known.[12]

A second factor working against TTRPG players trying to come up with ideas relates to **motivation losses**. This is the broad term describing how some people in a group will sit back and let others do the work if they can get away with it or if they feel that it doesn't matter.[13] **Social loafing** is a related concept where people ride the coattails of more motivated, higher-performing teammates. If you've ever seen a fellow player disappear into the kitchen or take out their phone while everyone else participates in one of these "what do we do?" debates, you've seen the consequences of motivation loss and social loafing.

The third and biggest reason why teams don't brainstorm as well as individuals is called **production blocking**. In a group setting, only one person can effectively share their ideas at a time, which blocks others from sharing theirs until they can take a turn.[14] We don't have the mental capacity to talk and listen at the same time, much less so when several people are involved. It also takes attention and thought to listen to and make sense of others' ideas, which are mental resources a person could use to come up with their own ideas.

All three of these problems become more acute as the size of the group increases.[15] The more people involved, the more you may worry about someone judging your ideas. The more people around the table, the more of a chance you have to coast and let others do the work. The more people that have ideas to share, the fewer opportunities each one of them has to do so. Also, these issues can be more severe in newer groups or when playing with strangers at a convention or a drop-in game at a game store. Groups can learn to trust one another not to judge and develop expectations that everyone takes turns, but that takes time and work.

What else can parties do to come up with more ideas about how to defeat a black dragon or rescue the town blacksmith? One lesson learned by researchers is that groups are most effective when brainstorming privately, and then coming together to evaluate, refine, and even criticize ideas. Anyone at the table, player or game master, could request that everyone write down their ideas privately for a few minutes. Do it on a pad of paper, on your phone, or even using chat if you're using a tool to play online. This will side-step issues like process blocking and concerns about judgment in the moment of idea creation. Then, when the group comes back together to share their ideas, some research suggests that players should ignore the "don't criticize ideas" advice and engage in critiques of ideas, but not of the people who came up with them.[16] Giving the group members permission to be critical gives them freedom to solve the problems and address shortcomings they identify.

This last point should also be the group's goal when it evaluates suggestions: combine their ideas into better ones and take inspiration from off-the-wall ideas to activate previously untapped veins of experience or knowledge.[17] Sometimes seeing things from a different perspective or in a different context can unlock new strategies and make you feel like you were wearing blinders before.

This process helps navigate a mental trap that a lot of TTRPG players might fall into: **functional fixedness**. This is a cognitive bias that keeps people from using an object for anything other than what it is normally used for. A 1945 paper in *Psychological Monographs* demonstrated this tendency with a simple challenge.[18] Subjects were given three little boxes, each with different contents: three small candles, some thumbtacks, and a handful of matches. Subjects were then asked to affix three candles to a door any way they could using only those items. Most of the subjects failed the task. They tried to use the thumbtacks to impale the candle onto the wall, but the wax crumbled. Others, a bit more creatively, tried to melt and then re-harden the wax so that it stuck the candle to the door, but that didn't work. Only a few overcame their functional fixedness bias towards the boxes that the items had come in and realized that they could dump out the contents, set the candles in the boxes, and then pin the boxes to the door. Nobody else thought of the boxes as anything other than containers. They were fixated on their obvious function.

I see this functional fixation happens all the time in *Dungeons & Dragons* and other TTRPGs, especially with the advent of higher quality, premade, more detailed maps and 3D printed terrain. For example, when players see stacks of barrels represented on a map, they may not think about them in any way except as decoration. They don't see them as cover from incoming arrows. They don't think of them as potential barricades. They don't see them as something that could be rolled down stairs to knock enemies prone. Or they may not see them at all if they're playing online with virtual tabletop software using line-of-sight tools that aggressively hide parts of the map from their view. We are less likely to think of creative uses for something absent from an otherwise highly detailed battle map, even when it makes narrative sense to be there. Say the fighter has a forest hag grappled with a headlock after the party kicked in the door to her decrepit woodland cottage. Wouldn't it be great if he could throw her into an oven, "Hansel and Gretel" style? Only this idea is less likely to occur to the player if they don't see an oven on the map and don't think to ask, "Is there an oven in this cottage?" They need to first overcome functional fixedness.

The brainstorming technique of thinking first alone and then together could help overcome functional fixation and other issues because when we hear ideas we haven't thought of, they trigger our associative memories.[19] We get the green light to speed down some other neural pathway and find a new connection. Give it a try the next time you hear those magic words, "So what do you want to do?"

WHAT YOU LEARNED IN THIS CHAPTER

- In the context of a team, "shared mental models" refers to members' understanding of what the team is supposed to do, the environment and rules it operates within, what each member is capable of doing, and the current state or capability of each member.
- Such team mental models should be both accurate and overlapping between party members to help them act and make predictions with minimal communication and overt strategizing.
- Good shared mental models shouldn't be taken as metagaming, which is a term for having a *character* act on something that only their *player* knows.
- Brainstorming can be hindered by fears of being judged by others, diminished motivation to participate when you're not held accountable, and the inconvenient fact that not everybody can simultaneously talk, listen, and think up their own ideas.
- Brainstorming individually and then bringing everyone's ideas together to debate and spur new thinking can be much more effective than brainstorming as a group.
- Functional fixedness is a cognitive bias that could limit our brainstorming and creativity by keeping us from using an object for anything other than what it is normally used for.

HOW TO APPLY THIS CHAPTER TO YOUR GAME

- Familiarize yourself with the abilities and capabilities of your teammates' characters as well as their preferences and play styles.
- Don't zone out when it's not your turn; keep track of major changes in other characters' statuses, capabilities, and actions so that you can be ready to combo or support them.
- Volunteer to play someone's character when they miss a session (if that's okay with them) or ask to control party henchmen and sidekicks to better develop your mental models.
- Engage is after-action debriefings with other players where you discuss how you could have worked together differently.
- Suggest that players write down ideas about how to tackle a problem or situation, then come together to discuss and generate new ideas.
- Think creatively about nonstandard uses for things your characters can interact with during an encounter or exploration to avoid the functional fixedness bias.
- Better yet, don't assume that because you don't see or hear about something, it's not there. Ask about it!

CHAPTER 12
WHICH IS BETTER: PLAYING IN-PERSON OR ONLINE?

They probably wish it weren't so, but the creators of the virtual tabletop (VTT) software Role20 benefitted from a lot of human suffering. Former college roommates Rolan Jones, Riley Dutton, and Richard Zayas were looking for a way to stay in touch after graduation. Jones had gotten into *Dungeons & Dragons* post-graduation and wanted a way to play with his old pals.[1] He wondered if people spread out across the country or even the globe could use computers to manipulate tokens on a map, access character sheets, and interact with each other through videoconferencing. Even better: what if all the rules one needed to run the game were right there in the software, indexed and searchable?

Dutton, an app developer, took his friend's wish to heart and whipped up a bare-bones way for them all to play *Dungeons & Dragons* over the internet.[2] Playing chess, wargames, and even TTRPGs through the mail and other primitive (yes, I said it, *primitive*) avenues of communication was a long-standing (if niche) practice at the time. But playing through the internet was novel in 2012, and the trio quickly realized that they had something special on their hands. They decided to take their fledgling product to the crowdsourcing service Kickstarter, where they could procure a bit of cash to make it legit. What was their goal? A modest $5,000. What did backers end up contributing? Almost $40,000.[3] Thus a software company was born and the first version of Roll20 was released to the public later the same year. It quickly attracted users, growing to one million players in 2015 and two million two years later. This coincided with (and helped fuel) the rise of the "actual play" scene, where groups would use Roll20 or similar software to record their games and stream them to online audiences via YouTube and Twitch. Roll20 then got a big boost in 2016 by acquiring a license to carry official *Dungeons & Dragons* material. Rulebooks, prewritten adventures, and supplements could be purchased and accessed directly through Roll20 so players didn't need to homebrew everything or stick to the free basic rules. At the same time, Roll20 competitors like Fantasy Grounds and Foundry were making their own licensing deals and experiencing similar growth.

VTTs continued to add new users over the next few years, and then things went nova in March 2020 when the COVID-19 pandemic curtailed in-person games all over the world. That's where "a lot of human suffering" enters the story, unfortunately.

At that time, I had been in a *Dungeons & Dragons* group that had been meeting in person every Friday night since 2011. But the game came to a stumbling halt once we went into quarantine. Like millions of other players, we turned to software like Roll20 and other VTTs to keep playing. We got on other services like Zoom or Discord to be able to see and hear each other while we played. By one estimate, online TTRPG play grew by 86% in 2020 alone.[4] The Director of Operations at Roll20 told the *LA Times* that requests for new accounts were so frequent during the first few days of quarantine that they thought they were under a distributed denial of service attack (also known as a DDoS attack) where attackers use automated tools to barrage websites with phony requests.[5] These requests, however, were real. Roll20 alone went on to double its user base between 2020 and 2022, growing to over ten million.[6] They weren't just scooping up existing *Dungeons & Dragons* players moving their games online, either. Brand new players were picking up the hobby as they looked for a way to connect with others at a distance. According to Wizards of the Coast, sales for the game leaped 33% in 2020, punctuating an already long trend of growth with a huge spike.[7]

All of this, coinciding with the rise of actual play streams and podcasts, means that for many players, online *Dungeons & Dragons* is the only *Dungeons and Dragons* they have ever seen or known. What experiences do virtual players have relative to in-person players? What does psychological research say about the effects of playing for three or more hours at a time using telecommunication tools like Zoom and Discord, especially when many of us stare into the same webcams all week for virtual work or classes? Are the friendships that you create and maintain through virtual games different from those formed by going to someone's house and meeting with them in person? These are the kinds of questions that we can draw from psychology research to answer in the rest of this chapter.

THREE LEVELS OF VIDEO CALL EXHAUSTION

Whether it's through Zoom, Discord, or the features built into a VTT, players need a way to communicate when playing virtually. And it's amazing how well this technology works and how low the barrier to entry is. That said, it's not the same as being together in person. Lacking access to the subtleties of face-to-face communication, many groups have more trouble taking turns when playing over video calls, much less audio-only calls. People talk over one another. It's harder to tell if other players are engaged or paying attention. If the game master asks a question, we may be unsure at whom the question is directed. It can be exhausting because requires extra mental resources to deal with these things throughout a three-to-five-hour online gaming session. These mental resources are even more scarce for those of us who already spent all week on video calls for work or school.

One bit of good news is that some researchers have taken note of this. Since the COVID-19 pandemic, Jeremy Bailenson, a professor at Stanford University, has started a line of research into what he calls "**Zoom fatigue**," which is a term that can be applied to the use of any videoconference technology.[8] It describes the sense of exhaustion and fuzzy-headedness that comes from staring at video conference calls for hours on end, asking if people can hear us, telling Bob that he's on mute, and shouting "KITTY!" whenever a pet cat wanders across someone's background.

Bailenson and other researchers contend that most of the reasons for Zoom fatigue are due to the extra mental resources needed to make sense of interactions that happen in a context that our ancestors never had to deal with. He repeatedly cautions that this is a new research area and that his ideas should be treated as mere theories in need of empirical testing, even though his ideas stem from existing research in psychology, sociology, and communications theory. That caveat aside, Bailenson proposes four possible causes for Zoom Fatigue: weird eye gaze, the cognitive load of dealing with unfamiliar nonverbal behaviors, reduced mobility, and protracted gazing into what is effectively a mirror.

First, close-up eye gaze has to do with how awkward it can feel seeing people interact with video conference calls. Mostly because of the size of their faces and the way they constantly seem to be staring at *you* when they're simply looking at their screen. If you were standing before someone in person and wanted to get close enough to make your face appear as big as it does on a typical video call, you would have to stand just a few inches away as you talk to them. This may be fine for those you're intimate with, like your husband or your child, but it feels like a violation of social norms when it happens with someone from a different family tree. What's more, it's awkward for people to stare at us directly in the eyes the entire time we're conversing. Because most people on a video call focus their gaze on their webcam, it looks like *every person* on the call is staring at us. And for each of these people, it also looks like everyone is staring at *them*, too. Dealing with these violations of social norms can take mental effort, even if it's subconscious.

Second, Bailenson notes that using video conference technology taxes your mental resources death by a thousand cuts because of all the little things you have to fiddle with and the extra effort needed to compensate for lost **nonverbal communication**.[9] This includes hand gestures, tone of voice, facial expressions, eye contact, posture, and any kind of person-to-person communication that relies on anything other than words. Besides adding context and additional information to the communications, these behaviors serve to create a sense of intimacy and immediacy between those communicating.[10] Such cues are much harder to perceive in video calls, which contributes to fatigue when we have to squint, ask clarifying questions, request that people repeat themselves, and slow things down to make sure we all understand.[11] And that's if the nonverbals are available at all; some things like posture or most hand movements are unreadable when you can only see a person from the chest up, and as mentioned earlier, making sense of eye contact or gaze is all but impossible. Research has shown that improving nonverbal behaviors between team members whose communication is mediated by technology can improve their collective problem-solving abilities.[12]

Third, Bailenson notes that video calls are fatiguing simply because we don't tend to get up and move around during them. When on a phone call you can stand up, stretch, walk around, and even wander into another room as long as you take the phone with you. When playing a TTRPG face-to-face, it's normal to occasionally stand up to stretch or stroll into the kitchen to refill your drink while still being able to hear what's going on with the game. You also need to regularly stand and reach across the table to nudge your mini around the battle map or reach a bowl of snacks. But stepping outside your camera's field of view during virtual games sometimes causes everyone to wonder if they lost you; it's as if you had just stopped existing.

Finally, Bailenson mentions the psychological effects of staring into the mirror that is a video call's "self-view." That is, the little square among a collage of other little squares that shows you to you. We're not used to seeing ourselves for such long periods and this self-view can gobble up our attention and focus. Research has found that looking into mirrors creates heightened self-monitoring.[13] This means that people who see their reflection tend to think about how other people are evaluating their behaviors and thus tend to be more honest and less likely to lose themselves to the bad influences of a crowd. Self-monitoring has costs, however. Some recent research has shown that feeling all that extra scrutiny on our faces can heighten anxiety about our appearance, which itself can be mentally draining over time.[14] That same research suggests that this effect is stronger for women and minorities. The topic of seeing yourself is even more complex for TTRPGs given the recommendations made in Chapter 5, where I discussed embodied cognition and the use of props and costumes to help you get into role-playing. It stands to reason that seeing a video of yourself dressed as or emoting like your character could help you identify with them and role-play. So you might want to turn on your webcam and your self-view if that's your goal, but at the same time doing so could be distracting and mentally taxing.

How do you deal with all this? Bailenson has several suggestions.[15] First, don't maximize the size of the video call app so that other people's faces don't feel in *your* face. Turn off your self-view if you notice fatigue or distraction setting in, then get up and move around while still within range of your microphone. Eschew marathon video calls that go on forever, or at least pepper them with breaks away from the screen. Do a one-time audit for your video setup where you improve the lighting, camera angle, and background to look decent. While you're at it, establish some norms around nonverbal behaviors like raising your hand to speak or being sure to explain when you're joking or impatient instead of relying on the nonverbal cues that would normally communicate such things.

But let's say you master playing *Dungeons & Dragons* via video call and your group starts to gel. Maybe you make all these friends online but never lay eyes on them in person. My Wednesday night group right now consists of an old high school friend and three of his friends. They all live hundreds of miles from me. My Friday night group started local and in-person, but we moved to virtual during the COVID-19 pandemic and stayed that way after three of them moved across the country. Are the friendships that we develop or maintain in situations like these the same as the relationships we have with people we see in person?

 ## ARE ONLINE GAMING FRIENDS THE SAME AS OFFLINE ONES?

Since the late 1990s, many researchers have been interested in what effect being online has on our offline lives. The less scientifically-minded pundits gasp breathy warnings and ask "Won't somebody think of the children?" But there's a lot of good work, too. The mainstream popularity of virtual tabletops and *Dungeons & Dragons* is too recent a phenomenon to inspire any research, but while we wait for a supervillain to hold the world hostage with a weather dominator and demand such research,[16] I think we can extrapolate from some of the studies that have been done on online social spaces, especially video games. In particular, we can look at the effect of interacting with people online versus offline in terms of what kinds of social capital are generated.

Social capital is often conceptualized by sociology and psychology researchers as the resources that we acquire from being members of a group, community, or institution.[17] This capital varies widely depending on who we're talking about, but examples include helpful information, emotional support when your weekly game gets canceled, social support in the face of tragedy, use of a truck to move some furniture, a place to stay while you're in town, or having someone cover a dinner bill when you leave your wallet at home. Social capital is unambiguously a positive outcome and tends to be self-perpetuating in that you create it by being in situations where you benefit from it.[18] Researchers have broken social capital down into two types: bridging and bonding.

Bridging social capital is formed through loose connections like those you typically get from a social club, a church, or a classroom. These kinds of connections are weaker. They're casual. They're a former classmate as opposed to your best friend from college. They're also numerous and tend to expose you to people who differ from you in important ways by connecting you to different networks that you would never otherwise encounter. Relative to relationships that create bonding social capital, people forming these connections tend to have different interests, values, worldviews, and personalities. Maybe not *radically* different, but different enough to form bridges between you and those other groups of people so you can access different kinds of social capital. This type of social capital doesn't have a whole lot to offer in terms of emotional support or big favors, but if you want access to information you don't already have or an introduction to a potential romantic partner, bridging relationships will often deliver.[19]

Bonding social capital, on the other hand, tends to come from much closer, more intimate relationships. Familial relations are the go-to example here, but bonding social capital also comes from close friendships and perhaps long-term mentors or teachers. Also you and me, I like to think, because you're pretty great. These relationships are fewer in number, but more intense and more lucrative in terms of the social capital they generate, at least in some ways. Bonding relationships are good for emotional support and tangible capital like money and favors. You'll have better luck asking your sister-in-law to check in on your dog while you're on vacation than someone you would describe as "a co-worker" or "the clerk from the convenience store."

All of this suggests a question: which type of social capital are you more likely to build when playing games like *Dungeons & Dragons* through a VTT, as opposed to in person? One study surveyed several hundred people and found that a lot depends on how easy it is to join the group and whether it's in-person or virtual.[20] If you found an online group through a message board or through your VTT's "Looking for Group" feature, it probably has a relatively low barrier for entry. You give the right answers to some basic questions like "Are you a psychopath yes or no?" and you're in. If turns out that everyone in the group is weird but not the type of weird you're looking for, you can leave just as easily. This research also found that when communities are easy to join and easy to leave, they tend to offer shallower relationships but exposure to more people and different kinds of people, especially in online communities.[21] In other words, online communities with low barriers to entry tend to provide bridging social capital, while offering less opportunity for bonding social capital.

A different study looked at over 800 e-sports video game competitors and gathered data on how physically close they were to each other, how embedded they were in each other's social networks, and how familiar they were with each other.[22] They found that when players were physically near their teammates and interacted with them in person (as opposed to only online), they were more likely to report generating bonding social capital. So it might be with *Dungeons & Dragons* players who get together in person. The study also found that social distance—how connected team members were and how often they interacted with each other—strongly predicted bridging capital because those interactions created opportunities to meet and interact with others in the community.

Can you generate bonding social capital from online interactions? Yes, but it is less likely because finding a tightly knit group to play with in person often requires that you all have at least one interest or person in common and you often rely on one another for tangible necessities like a place to play. In other words, in-person groups are harder to form and when they do form people tend to feel a sense of obligation and commitment to others. Face-to-face games also require players to live within driving distance of each other, which opens up possibilities for social capital that are absent when players live three time zones away.

REASONS WE PLAY ONLINE (OR NOT)

Finally, it's worth mentioning that a lot of research about people's choice to spend time online has focused on reasons and outcomes that I don't think are relevant to playing *Dungeons & Dragons* through VTTs. One such model is called **social displacement theory**, which holds that online gaming is problematic because if you're busy playing *Fortnite*, that gobbles up time that could be spent in wholesome, in-person activities like barbershop quartets or flash mobs.[23] This seems less relevant to playing TTRPGs online, which is as social an activity as anything it could displace. Even when playing through a VTT, you're seeing and hearing your fellow players, talking to them, collaborating with them, and getting to know them. But social displacement theory's genesis occurred during the early days of the mainstream internet and social media (the fabled age of the late 1990s) and some of its defenders explicitly omit the social aspects that eventually evolved.

This is unfortunate because there could be something there worth looking at, according to another theory of internet usage. **Social compensation** theory holds that you're just too socially inept to play games in person. Well, it's more polite than that and it doesn't single you out personally, but that's the gist. Some people aren't comfortable establishing relationships face-to-face. Yet, being human, they still crave such connections. For people like this, online interactions offer an attractive alternative because such environments compensate for the person's social shortcomings or hangups. As already mentioned, many online communities are easy to join and easy to leave.[24] You can lurk without expectations to participate until you have something to add. The structure of online spaces like video games offers rules for social interaction that are easier to understand and follow. You can worry less when you open up and share information about yourself because your reputation is limited to that space. Some of these characteristics also explain why playing *Dungeons & Dragons* through a VTT instead of finding an in-person group is more attractive to a subset of fans. That said, I will return to the role TTRPGs can play in developing social skills in Chapter 16.

Having the option to play TTRPGs online is fantastic despite everything said earlier in this chapter about how video calls can make communication more difficult, how playing online can be more exhausting, and how it often fails to build certain kinds of social capital. Because every group's situation is different, one could argue that any game of *Dungeons & Dragons* is better than no game of *Dungeons & Dragons*. One study systematically analyzed over 1,300 posts made to Reddit during the COVID-19 pandemic while players were transitioning from in-person play to online.[25] While many players complained about having to adapt to new technologies, others found platinum linings in the cloud. VTTs made it easier to schedule and find more time to play. Private, text-based communication made it easier for game masters to share secrets with individual players or role-play a sentient magic item that telepathically communicates with one player without the rest of the party hearing it. Some VTTs automate tasks like applying modifiers to dice rolls or making saving throws, which make parts of the game run more smoothly and quickly. It's easier for game masters running virtual games to create, find, and display assets like maps, artwork, and character tokens. Integrated tools allow players to track hit points, spell slots, and other resources with the click of a button. Many VTTs offer digital, searchable, and shareable versions of the rules that are easier to use than rulebooks.

I could go on, but you get the idea. Playing TTRPGs online is a great option with some advantages and some downsides. Hopefully, this discussion gave you some ideas about how to enhance the former and mitigate the latter.

WHAT YOU LEARNED IN THIS CHAPTER

- The recent, mass adoption of online play has been a boon to the TTRPG industry in general and virtual tabletop products in specific, but it's a different experience in some important ways.
- Zoom fatigue is a term that refers to increased exhaustion and mental drain that results from spending more time than we're used to using video call software of any kind.
- Research on this type of fatigue is still in its infancy, but what exists suggests that it may be due to close-up eye gaze, the cognitive load of dealing with unfamiliar nonverbal behaviors, reduced mobility, and protracted gazing into what's essentially a mirror.
- Social capital is the collection of resources that we acquire from being members of a group, community, or institution.
- Bonding social capital tends to provide more emotional support and tangible favors.
- Bridging social capital tends to provide more connections and exposure to different people and more varied ideas.
- Evidence suggests that online activities create more bridging social capital and less bonding.
- Some, though not all, people may be attracted to online spaces because the nature of interactions in such spaces compensates for their anxiety or weaker social skills.

HOW TO APPLY THIS CHAPTER TO YOUR GAME

- Reduce Zoom fatigue by turning off your camera or at least your self-view so you don't self-monitor as much.
- You can also try going audio-only, or minimizing the video call app so you only bring it up when you want to or need to see other players.
- Create and practice norms for things like taking turns, interrupting others, and dealing with limited access to nonverbal cues.
- Err on the side of overexplaining yourself and compensating for the lack of nonverbal communication.
- Get up and move around during the game while also calling for 10-to-15-minute breaks when everyone gets up and moves away from the computer.
- If you're looking for an online game, put yourself out there and don't be afraid to try out games with people of different backgrounds, races, genders, ages, and outlooks. You may end up building some valuable bridging social capital, not to mention making a friend or two.

CHAPTER 13

DOES CREATING A GAME WORLD MAKE IT MORE FUN TO PLAY IN?

The astronomer and great science communicator Carl Sagan once famously quipped, "If you wish to make an apple pie from scratch, you must first invent the universe." The joke is that truly starting from scratch means that you have to construct the building blocks of the building blocks of the building blocks, all the way back to whatever existed before there was *anything*. Sagan's quote came to me years ago when my *Dungeons & Dragons* group wanted to start a homebrew campaign from scratch. This meant that our game master, Eric, couldn't simply buy the equivalent of a store-bought apple pie in the form of an adventure or campaign setting that someone else had written. Instead, we assumed he was going to have to make the universe from scratch starting with a blank page. Creating a whole campaign setting from nothing is not only time-consuming, but it also pressures the game master to conjure up something that appeals to all the players and takes all their preferences and desires into account. That's rough.

There are many potential ways to haul oneself over this hurdle, such as borrowing and modifying many pieces from other campaigns or works of fiction. Or you could create a "spiral" campaign where you start the party in a small town, flesh that place out, and then have the characters spin out to neighboring areas that the game master creates on the fly. Or you could heavily modify someone else's world. Our game master chose a different solution. He came to the group armed with a printout of a little-known system called, *Dawn of Worlds: A Cooperative System for Creating Fantasy Worlds*. Created in 2005 by N. Bob Pesall and eight other collaborators, *Dawn of Worlds* aimed to turn the process of creating a fantasy world into part of the game. According to the rules, a group of people should start by gathering around a big sheet of paper. Someone then sketches out a continent or two, and then everyone gets busy playing the gods, whose job it is to shape the emerging world. In each round, players roll dice to accrue points representing their power to affect all of creation. The system has a table of options for how to exercise this power, including actions like shaping landmasses, altering climates, raising cities, casting cities down into ruin, creating new peoples to populate the world, spawning religious movements, and even unleashing dramatic catastrophes such as plagues, meteor strikes, or earthquakes.

My group had a blast using the system. In the first round, someone plopped an ancient, sprawling forest down onto the map. Then someone else populated it with a tribe of xenophobic halflings. On one of my turns, I created the great port city of Asmar, ruled by guild houses, clairvoyant wizards, and a conniving merchant king. In the next round, someone else injected a social movement into my city that made it a crime to use divine magic or practice religion. Then, on the other side of the map, another player invoked the system's "create catastrophe" power so that hordes of undead erupted from a mountain that generations of dwarves had used as a burial hall. And on and on we went until we had a campaign setting complete enough to get started.

The whole process was fun and engaging, thanks in no small part to the fact that all of us were involved and we all got to put our touches on the game world. We got to build on each other's work, modify it, shape it, and extend it. As a result, we were all excited to play in that world and several of us lobbied to sit behind the game master's screen and run adventures. In this way, our world and the process we used to create it emblemized one thing that's often great about TTRPGs: they feature co-creation and collaboration. Even if you don't create your apple pie from scratch, these games require you to riff off of others, work with the game master to hash out backstories, and decide which parts of the world will be filled in with fine detail and which parts will remain rough sketches because the party decides to go to one but not the other. On a moment-to-moment scale, every answer to the question of "What do you want to do?" is also an act of co-creation that defines the story you tell and the characters in it. It's not by accident that we value and enjoy worlds or stories that bear our fingerprints. Research on the psychology of co-creation tells us much about how you should approach co-creation in your games if you want to be a better and happier player.

BUILDING APPRECIATION

One famous psychological effect, which came into play when my group used *Dawn of Worlds* to build our campaign setting, takes its name from a Swedish home goods and furniture store known for making its customers assemble their purchases. **The Ikea effect** holds that we tend to like things more if we've expended effort to create them.[1] When you buy a bookshelf from Ikea, it comes in pieces with bags full of wooden dowels, screws, Allen wrenches, assembly instructions, and what may seem like a few too many umlauts. But put that thing together and according to research on the Ikea effect, it might feel more like *your* bookshelf than if you had bought it pre-assembled. While Ikea is a familiar example of this phenomenon, I prefer a different line of products whose creator has fully leaned into this effect: Build-A-Bear Workshop. A common sight in shopping malls all around America, Build-A-Bear stores invite kids to put together their own bespoke stuffed animals by choosing from base animal types, clothes, and accessories. Kids then decide how stuffed they want their creations to be, ranging from floppy to firm. Right now I'm looking at one of my teenage daughter's Build-A-Bear creations, a beige rabbit she named Bun Bun. She has loved Bun Bun dearly ever since she put him together as a young child. I asked her how much I would have to pay her to buy Bun Bun from her and throw it in a wood chipper, but she wouldn't give me an answer beyond "What are you talking about?" Even though Build-A-Bear creations are expensive and the company reliably convinces its customers to do work normally reserved for assembly line workers, kids love their stuffed animals because of the effort and customization choices, the memories of which are indelibly tied to each fluffy creation.

The Ikea effect (or Build-A-Bear effect, if you prefer) *feels* true, but is it real? One group of researchers set out to answer that question empirically with the help of origami frogs.[2] The experimenters set up a table in a student center and invited people passing by to learn origami. Those who agreed were given a set of instructions on how to make an origami frog (or a crane, if they preferred) and a sheet of paper with which to do it. Once finished, the subjects were asked to say how much they would be willing to pay for their own creation. As part of the same experiment, the researchers had a stock of pre-folded origami animals and then asked other subjects how much they would pay for one of those essentially identical creations. The key difference between the two groups, of course, was whether the person had gone through the intricate and demanding process of creating the little papercraft critter themselves or if it had come premade. What the researchers found was that those in the build-it-yourself condition were willing to pay over *four times as much* for the origami frog relative to those who had the chance to buy a premade one. The researchers found similar results with other do-it-yourself products like Lego sets.

Why does this mental bias occur? Researchers have pointed out several possible answers. One of the most popular is a specific kind of **cognitive dissonance.** This is the psychological phenomenon that describes how we don't like having two competing thoughts or opinions in our heads at once.[3] For example: "I voluntarily spent a lot of time making this origami frog" and "This origami frog is trash." When we try to hold thoughts that seem mutually exclusive in our minds at the same time, it's unpleasant and creates a bit of stress. It might even threaten our sense of self if the thoughts are about us and qualities about ourselves that we think are important. People go through all kinds of impressive mental gymnastics to avoid cognitive dissonance, but the go-to move is usually to change one of the conflicting beliefs. Since changing our memories about things we have done requires significant self-delusion, we usually turn to changing our opinions or judgments about things. For example, convincing ourselves that we did not spend four hours co-creating a *Dungeons & Dragons* campaign setting might be hard given the evidence of our memories and a world map with our handwriting on it. But obliterating the thought that all that work generated bad results is much easier to change and lets us avoid cognitive dissonance. This change need not be conscious and will often not be. But it is a common bit of mental gymnastics. Some researchers refer to these kinds of effects as **effort justification** when they specifically involve not wanting to think that time and effort were not worth the results.[4] The juice must always be worth the squeeze. If it's not, then you're not appreciating the juice enough. What sucker spends all that time squeezing fruit only to end up with tart, pulpy juice? Have you tried appreciating the juice more?

Another hypothesized reason for the Ikea effect is simple: making things makes us feel competent. It feels good to exercise our skills and to create something where there wasn't anything before. Anybody who has created a piece of art, grown a garden, written working computer code, typed out a character backstory, or engaged in any other act of creation probably knows the feeling. As we saw in Chapter 1, feeling competent is a basic psychological need that motivates us to engage in voluntary activities and it's part of what makes playing games enjoyable. The results of one study support this explanation in a backhanded way. The researchers first reduced participants' sense of competence by making them feel stupid in the face of difficult questions like:

> You have 4 coins. Three of the coins are normal, but one of them is heads on both sides. You pick a coin at random without looking. The coin you pick has heads on one side. What are the odds that if you flip the coin over, the other side will be tails?[5]

Does trying to answer that question make you feel like a dumb-dumb? Would successfully assembling an Ikea bookcase make you feel better? The researchers predicted that such an act of furniture-based creation would indeed make you feel better and that such a feeling of competence would magnify the Ikea effect. They were right: 58% of the study's participants said they would prefer to assemble the bookshelf themselves, relative to 33% in a group that was not asked the question above but instead was primed to feel competent by a question that most children could answer. The Ikea effect happens, at least in part, because making efforts and then seeing the outcomes makes us feel competent. And if we need to boost our sense of competence, creating something is a good way to get it. (In case you were wondering, the correct answer to the above question about the coins is 66.7%. Only 22% of the study's participants got it correct.)

Finally, the Ikea effect may also happen because we're biased in favor of ourselves. Part of our "psychological immune system" or **optimism bias** that helps us maintain a positive image of ourselves is a tendency to overvalue things specific to us. This is the same phenomenon that causes us to overestimate our ability so that we can maintain that positive self-image, which can then cause us to inflate the value of our creations. We focus on the strengths and ignore the flaws. We remember the cool parts of our character's backstory and forget the tired cliches. We're above average, shouldn't the things we work on be as well?[6]

So the Ikea effect may explain why I and my fellow players were so excited about that campaign that we co-created. We tend to overvalue things that we put effort into relative to equivalent creations from someone else. Putting our stamp on the campaign setting likely also made it feel like we owned, or at least co-owned, that world. Touching or interacting with something has been shown to increase perceptions of ownership,[7] and we spent hours interacting with our new creation. With a sense of ownership comes another bias that affects how awesome we think something is.

THIS IS MY DUNGEON: THE ENDOWMENT EFFECT

Once we own something, we tend to think it's worth more than other people think it's worth. This is known as **the endowment effect,** and it's surprisingly easy to trigger. Researchers at Duke University illustrated this cognitive bias in a clever experiment involving baseball tickets. When the supply of tickets to Duke's Blue Devils basketball games outstrips demand, fans are invited to enter a random lottery for the right to buy them. One season, researchers reached out to those who had won tickets in such a lottery and asked them how much they would be willing to sell them for. At the same time, the researchers contacted those who had wanted to buy the tickets but hadn't been lucky enough in the lottery. The researchers asked these people how much they'd be willing to pay for the same tickets. This meant they had two groups of basketball fans that were identical except that one group had tickets and the others didn't. Yet on average, those who had the tickets wanted an average of $1,400 to part with them while those who were looking for tickets were only willing to hand over an average of $170 for them. Same tickets, same game, both groups were taken randomly from the same population of fans.[8]

So it is with other things we feel like we own, be it coffee mugs, campaign settings, or characters in a TTRPG. To the extent that we feel ownership of something, we value it more relative to those who don't feel they own part of it. If my group had a new player come in weeks after we went through the session of campaign setting creation and ownership, they probably would not feel vested in that imaginary world and would not value it more than any other homebrew or prewritten adventure. Players and game masters in *Dungeons & Dragons* or other TTRPGs can take advantage of psychological phenomena like the Ikea effect and the endowment effect by engaging in co-creation and allowing people at the table to feel a sense of ownership and effort when it comes to the game.

 LEVERAGING THE CO-CREATION AS A PLAYER

Besides a campaign-building exercise like the one described at the top of this chapter, TTRPG players can be on the lookout for other ways to seize a sense of co-creation and co-ownership—during character creation, for example. Using pre-generated characters is useful for one-shot adventures where time is limited or to avoid overwhelming new players, but players don't tend to get attached to them as they do to characters they make themselves. I once played a pre-generated barbarian at a gaming convention and laughed it off when that character was turned to stone and died. But when Melcurio, a tiefling warlock/paladin I had created, was obliterated by an unlucky die roll, I was upset and petitioned the game master to contrive a way for him to be resurrected. I valued one character way more than the other because for one of them I had come up with my own character concept, backstory, and personality.

Players don't have to do all the creation themselves, though. If you want everyone at the table engaged, co-creation should be the goal. Deciding that your dwarven wizard is on the run from parents bent on her taking over the family mining business is great. But if the game master suggests that you later find out it was the campaign's villain who contrived your character's departure so he could take over mining operations and unleash a terror buried beneath the family mines, then that's great, too! Let go of whatever contradictory bits of backstory you have and let the game master in on the creation.

I once had an opportunity to do this in a game where my swashbuckling rogue's ship was boarded by pirates. The game master looked at me, dropped a miniature meaningfully down on the battle map, and said, "You look across the gangplanks and see none other than your old captain grinning at you maliciously!"

I didn't know my character had any old captains of note, but I leaned into it. "Peg-Face Pete?" I asked. "The most dangerous wood golem to sail the seven seas?"

The game master paused, scratched something out in his notes, and then jotted down this new development. "Yes!" he exclaimed, and we then went on to have a great character development beat.

Game masters aren't the only ones that players should strive to co-create with. Players are also at the table waiting to be let in on the creation fun. Again, this can start with character creation and backstory. Rather than simply rolling dice, suggest to other players that they have existing relationships, such as the gruff fighter serving as your character's loyal bodyguard after your character's fast-talking got the two of you out of trouble. Got two halflings in the group? What if they were cousins, with one tagging along to protect the other and always trying to talk him into returning to their pastoral homeland? Not only does this provide hooks for future role-playing, but it also gives each player a stake in the other's story, so that they will value and care for the other's character more as the adventure plays out.

 LEVERAGING CO-CREATION AS A DUNGEON MASTER

Of course, most creation duties ultimately fall to game masters, but that means they have the most opportunities to leverage these psychological phenomena related to co-creation and co-ownership. One basic technique is to simply answer questions by lobbing them back at players. If the party enters the bar and wants to find local guides to help investigate rumors about nearby woods overrun by monsters, that could catch an unprepared game master off guard. So while you're scrambling to think of what information guides might provide, you could say "Yeah, you find two of them drinking together. Why don't *you* tell everyone their names and what they're like?" Suddenly, you've got two moderately fleshed-out NPCs that the party can interact with. They will also likely remember details about the pair because they helped create them. A similar approach can be taken in creating environments; ask players to describe whatever tavern, shop, stable, abandoned tower, or forest glade the party has just traipsed into. You may need to revise their descriptions (no, there is *not* a huge pile of gold sitting in the middle of the farmer's field), but that's easier than starting from scratch and details from players let you know what they find interesting and what you might be able to riff on as you build a story together.

One other trick along these lines is asking players to name an identifying characteristic of enemies during combat. If you have Kobold A, Kobold B, and Kobold C assaulting the party, you could label them in the initiative tracker and on the battle map as such. But a more interesting approach would be to ask players to come up with one physical characteristic for each kobold that starts with that enemy's letter. So one player could declare that Kobold A is "Arrow Kobold" because its shield is bristling with arrows. Another player might suggest that Kobold B is "Belt Kobold" because it's wearing a huge belt with an ornate buckle. Kobold C, of course, is the "Calcium Kobold" because it's chugging milk while maintaining eye contact with the party's wizard. You're guaranteed to get some wise-cracking with this method, but it's a fun, low-stakes way to get players involved in creating memorable encounters.[9]

There is one caveat to these kinds of requests that the savvy game master (or player trying to do the same thing) should keep in mind: when you ask for player involvement in coming up with descriptions for NPCs, details on environments, characteristics of monsters, or any other bits of world-building, you shouldn't frame it as asking for their *opinion* on what something should be.

Asking for opinions puts the other person in mind to find faults in your idea, which makes them feel distant and detached from you. Instead, if you can frame your request as one for *advice* on how things should be, players should be more likely to adopt a collaborative and cooperative mindset that feels more like a partnership. This tip is supported by a study that told participants about a new restaurant that was going to open up and then solicited either their advice or opinion about it.[10] Relative to those who were asked their "opinion," those who were asked to give "advice" were not only more likely to eat at the restaurant, but they also reported feeling a closer connection to the person soliciting input. This is, the researchers say, because getting in the mindset of providing advice creates perceptions of a closer, more collaborative relationship. Sometimes the advice framing doesn't make sense ("What's your advice on the barkeep's name?" is a weird question, for example) but, when possible, this is a good way to elicit players' input.

 WHAT YOU LEARNED IN THIS CHAPTER

- The Ikea effect happens when we overvalue something we helped create relative to identical, premade items.
- Cognitive dissonance describes how we will change what we think to avoid holding two mutually exclusive thoughts, opinions, or beliefs at the same time.
- Effort justification refers to overvaluing something to avoid considering that the time and effort you put into it was wasted.
- The endowment effect refers to how we tend to think something is more valuable once we own it.

 HOW TO APPLY THIS CHAPTER TO YOUR GAME

- As a player, seek out ways that you can get involved with the creation of your game's characters, lore, environments, and NPCs.
- Find ways to involve your character in other characters' backstories or motivations
- As a game master, solicit advice from your players about the names, appearance, and even characteristics of NPCs, enemies, or locations.
- On a grander scale, pull all the players together and go through a cooperative co-creation process for homebrew campaigns where everyone gets a chance to shape the world, its people, and its nature.

CHAPTER 14
WHY DO WE ESCAPE INTO IMAGINARY WORLDS?

A group of criminals once tried to use *Dungeons & Dragons* to escape Wisconsin's Waupun Correctional Institution.

They weren't *literally* using 20-sided dice to dig tunnels and hide their handiwork behind a picture of a sexy red dragon like with the poster of Rita Hayworth in *The Shawshank Redemption*. Nor were they using maps and minis to plan escape routes under the guise of battling orcs. Instead, back in 2004, a small group started *figuratively* escaping the drudgery of their prison lives by playing a game that let them imagine going somewhere fantastical and being someone else. An inmate named Kevin Singer organized the group and served as its game master, reconnecting with a love of the game that began long before his incarceration.[1] Singer ordered *Dungeons & Dragons* material through the mail and created a handwritten, 96-page homebrew campaign setting for the game. Using this material, he and three other inmates set aside potential rivalries and social stratification to go on quests, perform heroic deeds, and make believe during their limited recreation time—until the prison's "Disruptive Group Coordinator" Captain Bruce Muraski took note of Singer and his gaming group.

Fearing that the game was being used to organize gang activity, Muraski ordered a search of the players' cells and confiscated all of the *Dungeons & Dragons* material he found. He wasn't alone among his professional colleagues in breaking up inmates' games. In the May 2002 edition of *Dragon* magazine, Group Publisher Johnny Wilson penned an editorial about how other prisoners across the United States were having their *Dungeons &*

Dragons material, including issues of Wilson's own *Dragon* magazine, confiscated before it ever left the prison's mail room.[2] Wilson encouraged his readers to act via a letter-writing campaign to prison administrators. Kevin Singer, however, decided on a more direct path to justice. He sued Captain Muraski and the prison officials in court to get his stuff back.[3]

To make his case, Singer sought help from 15 of his fellow inmates who had played the game. He also called upon experts on TTRPGs, such as an officer in the Committee for the Advancement of Role-Playing Games, an international group dedicated to cataloging research on the benefits of *Dungeons & Dragons*. The inmates testified that to their knowledge, based on their collective 100 years of prison experience, no game of this type had been used to create or organize gangs. Scholars called upon to comment on the case extolled the many rehabilitative aspects of TTRPGs, including their positive effects on literacy, numeracy, social skills, and general rehabilitation.

The court seemed to listen to and understand Singer's arguments, but it ultimately sided with the prison officials, who pointed out that playing the game could encourage "addictive escape behavior." The court's decision didn't make it clear, at first, whether Muraski was talking about literal escape behaviors where players would use the game to plot an escape from the Waupun Correctional Institution, or if he was discussing a more psychological escape akin to daydreaming. Eventually, though, it became clear that he was concerned about both. According to the court:

> [Captain Bruce Muraski's] affidavit expressed concerns not only about gang behavior but also about potential inmate obsession with escape, both figurative and literal. He testified that D & D "could foster an inmate's obsession with escaping from the real life, correctional environment," placing both the legitimate penological goals of prison security and inmate rehabilitation in peril.[4]

In other words, among the prison officials' concerns was the possibility that using the game to take players' minds off their lives as prisoners ran counter to the punitive purpose of imprisonment.

And while most of us aren't serving prison time, we can empathize with the inmates and imagine how devastating it must have been to lose their ability to escape to a fantasy world, because that's at least part of why so many of us play *Dungeons & Dragons*. But does it work? Can we use TTRPGs to mentally escape our lot in the real world in favor of something better? And on whose side is the science—Kevin Singer's, who wanted to play to help rehabilitate and improve himself, or Captain Bruce Muraski's, who feared that such escape behavior would be addictive and interfere with players' capacity to come to terms with the real world and their mistakes within it?

ESCAPE VS. ESCAPISM

Escapism has gotten a bad rap in the psychology field. Until recently, **escapism** had been almost solely defined as avoiding unhappiness or stress by doing something else that lets you ignore or repress the root causes of those emotions. One of the earliest theories along these lines came from psychologist Roy Baumeister, who said that escapism is a need to get away from constant monitoring of our own actions, emotions, and thoughts by doing things that take our attention away from ourselves and fix it firmly on something else.[5] It's about avoidance, dissociation, and isolation, suggesting poor psychological well-being and the maladaptive, short-term dodging of reality, which could be better faced head-on. Baumeister's examples of escapist behavior include drug abuse, alcohol abuse, and gambling. Subsequent researchers have tossed in excessive use of media like television and the internet. Specifically in the context of games, much of the research on escapism has focused on excessive video game play (often couched in terms of addiction), where people try to leave their problems behind by shooting zombies, capturing control points, or crushing candy.[6]

That's not quite fair, though. While some people escape into gambling, binge-watching anime, or doing raids in *Final Fantasy XIV* to the detriment of their psychological well-being, others escape into video games, the internet, or *Dungeons & Dragons* in a healthy way. More relevant to the goals of this chapter is the question of whether you can swap the real world for that of a TTRPG in a way that makes you happy, nurtures your interests, and lets you come back to life outside the game better than you left it. The good news is that you can, depending on the circumstances and how you approach it.

Specifically, it depends on why you're trying to escape whatever is making you stressed and unhappy. Recent reconceptualizations of escapism posit that two motivations for escapist behaviors exist. One is what was described above: engaging with an activity or a piece of media to repress thoughts about your lousy job, your stressful home life, your failing grades, your dire financial situation, or anything else that causes you otherwise unbearable stress. By escaping into an imaginary world through reading, watching television, or playing games, a person can avoid ruminating on their real-life situation, set aside the negative emotions it presses upon them, and most importantly, do something besides beating *themselves* up through critical self-reflection. Frode Stenson from the Norwegian University of Science and Technology and his collaborators call this the **self-suppression** dimension of escapism.[7] In their research, they saw that people using games or other media in this way would be more likely to agree with statements like, "When I engage in my activity, I try to suppress my problems," or,

"When I engage in my activity, I try to prevent negative thoughts about myself."[8] If you're a level zero commoner in real life with lousy prospects for romance, financial stability, or a good career, it's tempting to dive into activities that allow you to ignore all that.

While published research to date on the use of games as a form of self-suppression is limited to video games and gambling, it's only an inferential hop to argue that playing and thinking about *Dungeons & Dragons* could be used in this way. The game isn't as constantly available as video games thanks to the involvement of other people and the scheduling challenges any player is probably familiar with, but players can think about the game at all hours and game masters can plan, prep, write, research, and craft constantly if they set their minds to it. And with the advent of online play, any TTRPG fan can find two, three, four, or more games a week to participate in if they want to. They may not all be perfect fits, but that's not the point. The point is that they could be using them to escape worse things. This is the escapism that prison officials at Wisconsin's Waupun Correctional Institution seemed to be worried that Kevin Singer and his fellow inmates were going to engage in. That with the help of a few character sheets and a 96-page, handwritten campaign guide, the inmates were going to perpetually inoculate themselves against the punitive consequence of their life choices and subsequent imprisonment.

But Singer seemed to have other ideas, based on the affidavits he submitted from scholars and other experts in the use of TTRPGs during his lawsuit. One of them, from the Committee for the Advancement of Role-Playing Games, argued that games of this type can have many effects that promote rehabilitation rather than undermine it. Frode Stenseng and his co-authors would probably agree, given how their research suggests a second type of escapism. This type can be good for you, or at least leave you better off than you were before your jaunt into an imaginary world. This second type of escapism happens when a person is interested in using an activity to bring about positive effects such as mastering the activity, improving their mood, and improving themselves. This **self-expansion** dimension of escapism is much more intentional and resembles a healthy coping strategy instead of self-suppression.[9] It is unrelated to addiction and excessive participation in an activity but is still characterized by the participant looking forward to the activity because of the enjoyment and personal growth it will bring. In Stenseg's research, people with this motivation to escape were more likely to agree with questions like, "When I engage in my activity, I try to get to know myself better," and, "When I engage in my activity, I am filled with positive energy that transfers to other parts of my life."[10]

In one study aiming to disentangle these two motivations for escape, researchers measured both self-suppression and self-expansion motivations in samples of video game players.[11] They found that those who played games to engage in self-suppression were more likely to express general negative moods and score higher on measures of a compulsive, unhealthy relationship with gaming. Those who played for self-expansion, however, did not report such negative moods nor did they seem to play games excessively to the detriment of other areas of their lives. Given this, the authors argue that failing to distinguish between these two motivations for escape could represent a failure to differentiate between healthy and unhealthy use of games.

What this comes down to is that your motivation for escaping into a game of *Dungeons & Dragons* matters. If your desire to escape is one-way—if you want to immerse yourself in a fictive world and never come back—then that repression isn't likely to lead to good outcomes.[12] But if you expect your escape to be a temporary round trip during which you seek to practice some skill, reflect upon who you are or who you could be, brighten your mood, and develop some ways to cope with those troubles waiting for you back home, that's far more adaptive. I've talked at length earlier in this book about strategies for self-determination, role-playing, and social interaction that you could employ. I will also discuss how TTRPGs can be used to develop other skills in Chapter 16.

Further research shows that escaping into a fantasy world via a good game of *Dungeons & Dragons* can have benefits even if you're dealing with mundane, everyday stress. Sometimes it's the perfect experience to help us get over a long week of work or school.

DUNGEONS, DRAGONS, AND RECOVERY

For most of us, great swaths of our lives follow the pattern of "work, rest, repeat." We labor for hours on end at school, in a job, or in the home, which drains us of mental and emotional resources. If you're lucky enough to be something fun like a professional game master or a game designer at Wizards of the Coast, that drain may be more of a slow leak but it still adds up for the majority of people. It's exhausting to deal with work obligations day after day. Research has found that this is especially true when one's work is characterized by two things. One is high job demands, which covers things like long hours, stressful responsibility, time pressure, and the absence of support from others. The other is a lack of control over our work, such as schedule setting or deciding how work gets done. In one study, researchers called thousands of Dutch citizens at random and asked them about their work and how they dealt with it.[13] The study found that to the degree that job demands were high and job control was low, people had a high

need for recovery. In other words, people eventually got so mentally and emotionally wrung out that they didn't want to do the work anymore.

When we get like this, we need more than a break. Sure, you could sit and stare at your feet from Friday night to Monday morning, but research on stress and recovery has shown that, counterintuitively, what we need to recover those lost mental and emotional resources is *more* activity. But it has to be an activity outside of work.[14] We go to class and study during the week then hit the gym or go for a run at night. We deal with angry customers Monday through Friday, then on the weekend we enjoy post-apocalyptic fiction where society has collapsed and no customers remain. We get the kids off to school and keep the household running during the day, then binge-watch anime at night. These leisure activities may take time, effort, focus, and even work, but research shows that they are refreshing because they are different from work.

However, not all recovery experiences are created equal. Some activities consistently help us recover from the demands of work more than others. One line of research suggests an ideal recovery experience provides four things:
1. Psychological detachment from work
2. Relaxation
3. Mastery experiences
4. Control

First is **psychological detachment**, which is a way of asking, "Have you tried *not* being at work? If so, have you also tried not *thinking* about being at work?" Because those two things are amazingly effective for recovery from stress. If an activity allows you to unplug (or "psychologically detach" in fancy psychology language) from work, it means you're distracted enough not to think about the work ahead of you or the work you've temporarily left behind. It lets you stop ruminating on your work responsibilities so you can turn your mind to other things. To the degree that we psychologically detach, we tend to have more positive emotions. We also feel less "activation," which is when our brains become aroused so that we pay close attention to our surroundings and get our neurons firing. Lower chronic activation also means less fatigue and stress-induced health problems.[15]

Playing games like *Dungeons & Dragons* helps facilitate psychological detachment. If you're focusing on playing the game, rolling your dice, interacting with other players (see Chapter 3) immersing yourself in the world (Chapter 4), or role-playing your character (Chapter 7), that leaves less space to obsess over work. While relatively passive activities like reading, watching television, or going for a walk can also help us detach from work, playing a game —especially a TTRPG—is a much more active undertaking and thus creates even more detachment than other options. This concept of psychological detachment also seems to harken back to the self-expansion dimension of escapism and the two concepts are often discussed together in the research. Players detach from work the same way that one detaches from any stressful situation, hopefully in a way that allows them to feel better once they come back to work.

The second feature of an ideal recovery experience is **relaxation**. The drain on our resources doesn't stop the second we cease working. There can be spillover that lasts hours. Relaxation helps that unspooling happen more quickly and it helps improve mood. It's a combination of good mood and that concept of "chilling out" or low activation discussed earlier. Using media of all kinds as a form of mood management has a long history. One early study on the use of television to manage mood gave over 100 people in the Chicago area little radio-activated devices, like "pagers" or "beepers" to those of you who remember such things, that could be remotely activated at random times.[16] When their pager went off, subjects were to note in a journal what they were doing at the time, as well as to answer a bunch of questions about their state of mind. The results consistently showed that when people sat down to watch a night full of television, they were in a bad mood. Rather than claiming that television causes bad moods, the researchers concluded that people watched television *in response to* being in a bad mood, as a way to relax and improve their emotional state.

Using media for mood management can be an effective and adaptive coping strategy.[17] The same principles should apply to a recovery activity like playing games. Such an activity can be emotional in different ways, but it most often makes people feel happy and excited. Again, while research in this area hasn't typically included tabletop games specifically, one study looked at the relationship between relaxation and playing video games. Unsurprisingly, they found that more time spent playing video games correlated with more self-reports of feeling relaxed and detached from work.[18] This sounds like the perfect monograph for a special issue of the *International Journal of "Well, DUH"*, but it's nice to know that these things are being backed up by science.

The third and fourth things that ideal recovery experiences provide have to do with qualities of *Dungeons & Dragons* that we've already thoroughly covered in earlier chapters. They are **mastery experiences** (Chapter 1) and **control** (Chapter 2). Playing TTRPGs provides constant opportunities to feel like you and your character are growing in power, skill, and competence. It also gives you an almost unparalleled level of control over your activity and the choices you exercise. You get at least some control over when you play a game, with whom you play, and how to play the game. Work rarely gives you those feelings of mastery and control, and if it does it doesn't do it consistently the way playing games does. Playing *Dungeons & Dragons* is a rejuvenating experience that satisfies basic psychological needs that work may not.

In sum, this model of stress recovery suggests playing games is an ideal experience because they're interactive, they require attention, and they help detach from work. And they both relax you and boost your mood. Not only that, playing games in general and *Dungeons & Dragons* in particular helps satisfy fundamental psychological needs for mastery and choice in ways that work often does not. But there's one more characteristic of TTRPGs that may make it preferable to other activities, even to playing video games: playing these games is inherently social. Research has shown an inverse relationship between the amount of social support one has and how likely one is to turn to games for recovery.[19] Because friends are awesome and social support can amplify how effective recovery experiences can be at getting us ready to face work again.

WHAT YOU LEARNED IN THIS CHAPTER

- Escapism has two dimensions: self-suppression and self-expansion.
- Self-suppression is trying to use activities to avoid thinking about the causes of stress and to avoid critical self-reflection. This is considered to be maladaptive and can lead to worse outcomes like lower psychological well-being and excessive engagement with the activity.
- Self-expansion is escaping to cope with the cause of stress, manage one's mood, and develop new skills or attitudes that make you feel better about yourself.
- Your reasons and motivations for engaging in escapism will largely drive which type you experience.
- Need for recovery is the need to replenish emotional and mental resources that are gobbled up by work of any type.
- A strong need for recovery is most likely when work demands are high (in terms of time, responsibility, and workload) and control over one's work is low.
- Activities outside of work are key to recovery. Those that provide psychological detachment, relaxation, mastery experiences, and control are the most effective.
- To the extent that we lack social support in our lives, recovery activities that provide such social interaction will also be effective.

HOW TO APPLY THIS CHAPTER TO YOUR GAME

- When you seek to escape into a game to leave your troubles behind, think about what insights and good feelings you can bring back with you on the return trip.
- Seek out TTRPG experiences that let you stop thinking about work, childcare, or the kinds of things you're responsible for. Shut up about work at the gaming table!
- Seek out experiences (or provide them if you're the game master) that let you develop a sense of mastery and autonomy about the game.
- Other research has found that physical activities (e.g., exercising or blacksmithing) are also wildly effective at recovery, so don't neglect those.

CHAPTER 15
DOES PLAYING *DUNGEONS & DRAGONS* TURN KIDS INTO DEVIL WORSHIPERS?

No.

CHAPTER 16

DOES PLAYING *DUNGEONS & DRAGONS* HELP US IMPROVE OUR SKILLS AND MENTAL HEALTH?

A lot of my childhood friends hid the fact that they played *Dungeons & Dragons*. Sometimes it was because of a parent's moral panic (see Chapter 15), but other times it was because some of our parents (and more than a few of our peers) thought it was a weird waste of time meant for introverted dorks with no social skills. Which is nonsense. Well, the "bunch of dorks" part may be true, but the current popularity of genre entertainment built around fantasy, science fiction, and superheroes is a balm for those of us burned by becoming early adopters. But the part about *Dungeons & Dragons* players having no useful skills, social or otherwise? That seems untrue as soon as you look at what people do when they play the game. I was luckier than some of my friends in that my parents took the time to leaf through my *Player's Handbook*, ask me what it was all about, and conclude that it was far from the worst thing a teenager could be doing. I distinctly remember my mother answering another mom's skepticism with, "Well, he keeps his nose stuck in those books, but at least I know he's reading and playing with friends."

She was right. TTRPG players not only have to read a lot, but playing such games requires that they exercise certain skills that are great to have outside of the game. The game requires math, applied logic, short- and long-term memorization, three-dimensional spatial skills, emotion regulation, and planning. Social skills flexed by TTRPGs include communication, collaboration, and reading the emotions of those around you through empathy and perspective-taking.[1] In this chapter, I'll review skills that TTRPGs might help us develop in the course of normal play. Plus, we will look at how some therapists use *Dungeons & Dragons* in therapeutic settings to help people with specific mental health diagnoses and development needs.

READING COMPREHENSION AND NUMERACY

Take a deep breath and read the following description of the Phantasmal Force spell from the 2014 *Dungeons & Dragons 5th Edition Player's Handbook*:[2]

2nd-level illusion

Casting Time: 1 action

Range: 60 feet

Components: V, S, M (a bit of fleece)

Duration: Concentration, up to 1 minute

You craft an illusion that takes root in the mind of a creature that you can see within range. The target must make an Intelligence saving throw. On a failed save, you create a phantasmal object, creature, or other visible phenomenon of your choice that is no larger than a 10-foot cube and that is perceivable only to the target for the duration. This spell has no effect on undead or constructs.

The phantasm includes sound, temperature, and other stimuli, also evident only to the creature.

The target can use its action to examine the phantasm with an Intelligence (Investigation) check against your spell save DC. If

DOES PLAYING *DUNGEONS & DRAGONS* HELP US IMPROVE OUR SKILLS AND MENTAL HEALTH?

the check succeeds, the target realizes that the phantasm is an illusion, and the spell ends...

That's not even the full spell description! It's only the first half, but it illustrates how complicated some of the rules can be and how much reading comprehension they demand of players. To use that spell you have to read the description and understand details like how it has to be cast on a target within 60 feet, that you have to be able to see the target, and that the target gets an Intelligence-saving throw—unless it's an undead or construct, in which case no saving throw is needed because the spell does not affect such creatures. You also must understand the boundaries of what your character can create with the spell (sized to fit in a 10-foot cube) and that creatures other than the target don't perceive the illusion. You have to understand when the illusion will end: 60 in-game seconds or when the target succeeds on an Investigation skill check. That's a lot of information, and it's only for one spell! Players may have dozens of spells available to them, and what's more, they must reference an entire book's worth of rules that are sometimes tricky to understand—multiple books if they're the game master. It is an impressive feat of literacy. I've played the game for decades, and I still struggle to understand the rules for grappling with another creature, for example.

Similar to literacy, *Dungeons & Dragons* and other TTRPGs require numeracy, otherwise known as skill with numbers and mathematics. Say you cast fireball on a pack of abyssal chickens, an actual *Dungeons & Dragons* monster that I promise I did not just make up. Roll eight six-sided dice. Add up the results of $5+2+1+5+4+2+5+3$. But these evil chickens only take 50% damage to fire thanks to their demonic nature, so half the damage, rounding down. They also get to make a Dexterity saving throw equal to 8, plus your proficiency bonus (2), plus your spellcasting ability score modifier (3), to take half of *that* damage. Two of them succeeded on that saving throw, so reduce their total damage by 75%. And make it quick because other people are waiting to take their turn. None of this is advanced algebra or calculus, but all the basic mathematical operations are constantly in play, and I've been at more than one table where the Pythagorean Theorem was invoked to figure out how far an arrow would have to travel to hit a creature flying 40 feet up and 100 feet away.

Getting kids and even adults to practice their reading and math skills in a traditional classroom can be difficult. Some people also have reading disorders. But practicing reading and math skills in the context of a TTRPG is fun, engaging, useful, and practical, so it can lead to improvements and build confidence when other interventions fail.[3] In one case study of seven teens who played *Dungeons & Dragons,* all participants reported that playing the game helped them improve their literacy skills. One even said that it helped him push past challenges posed by his dyslexia to read through entire rulebooks.[4] Other surveys have found that those who spend a lot of time playing TTRPGs also read more than others[5] (though whether the games led to more reading or the other way around wasn't tested).

LOGICAL REASONING AND PLANNING

Another mental skill exercised by TTRPGs is logical reasoning, which can be defined as arriving at a conclusion via rigorous thinking or the use of logic. It involves applying premises and then using logic to arrive at conclusions. In a game like *Dungeons & Dragons*, logical reasoning is required to decide when to quaff an invisibility potion, to exploit an enemy's weaknesses such as a troll's vulnerability to fire, or to figure out a way to cross an ice-covered bridge. Many spell and class abilities demand logical

DOES PLAYING *DUNGEONS & DRAGONS* HELP US IMPROVE OUR SKILLS AND MENTAL HEALTH?

reasoning, such as deducing that a lumbering zombie probably has a low dexterity score and could face plant if the Grease spell were cast at its feet. It would also be used to deduce that the zombie's prone position would make it harder for a distant archer to hit. Logical reasoning is also involved with interpreting complex rules, like whether a rogue can use their sneak attack ability if they are standing next to that prone, grease-covered zombie. But it's not only combat that requires logical reasoning. It can also come into play during exploration to bypass traps or in social encounters where players have to deduce NPC motivations or solve murder mysteries.

Relatedly, TTRPGs frequently tax players' planning skills and their ability to predict future states based on logical reasoning, knowledge of cause/effect chains, and probability.[6] Brash barbarians aside, thoughtful planning is often needed to adequately answer the game master's recurring query of "What do you want to do now?" During one adventure, my party was tasked with rescuing an NPC from a high-security prison without killing anyone. After prolonged discussion, we contrived a plan to disguise ourselves as kitchen staff and prison guards. We then planned to deliberately, but non-lethally, poison the NPC so that the party members posing as guards could relocate him to the infirmary, where it would be easier to extract him to a getaway skiff waiting at the nearby docks. This plan involved useful mental skills such as goal setting, anticipating the likelihood of future events, predicting obstacles, and breaking big tasks down into sub-tasks. And, when the plan went a bit wrong and the alarm was raised, the situation demanded that we adapt and enact contingency plans, like using the Arcane Lock scroll to bar the way of pursuing guards and covering our escape by enthusiastically tooting on a Horn of Fog —both of which we had smuggled into the prison in case of such a need.

COMMUNICATION

Dungeons & Dragons players must not only know how to read words from a rulebook, but also how to use their own words to communicate ideas, plans, and desires. Shoving miniatures around on a battle map and grunting at the game master only gets you so far. Sometimes our ideas and plans are complex, requiring a careful choice of words. Persuasion skills can be as important to players as they are to characters, as players may need to convince others at the table to go along with their plan, which is a different skill than simply describing the plan. Communication skills are also critical to describing how your character feels, reacts, or thinks, which can open up new vocabulary and new ways to relay your thoughts, emotions, and mental states outside of the game.[7]

Beyond diction, rhetoric, and self-expression, playing games like *Dungeons & Dragons* requires players to become comfortable with communicating with others. Frequently this involves talking to peers, which can be harrowing enough, but it may also involve interacting with people from different levels of power or status, like younger players talking to adults or newcomers of any age joining an established group of friends. TTRPGs provide a social scaffolding that can help players conquer anxiety about talking to other people, allowing them safe topics for conversation like the game, their character, and the events of the campaign. One survey of TTRPG players found that 73% of them developed friendships with fellow players to the point where they got together outside of the game sessions "often" or "very often."[8] Furthermore, their conversations drifted into topics outside of the game over time as they shared or developed other common interests.

COOPERATION AND COLLABORATION

As discussed extensively in Chapter 11, collaborating with others to do cool stuff is at the heart of *Dungeons & Dragons*. Given this, it's easy to see how the game gives players constant opportunities to practice teamwork. It's not a competitive game and players can only hog the limelight for so long before it (hopefully) wanders off to illuminate someone else. Players learn not only to compromise on what they want to do, but more often than not, they come up with win-win situations where everyone joins hands, sings together in harmony, and burns the bandit camp to the ground. Like other works of fiction with ensemble casts, *Dungeons & Dragons* campaigns are structured so that groups of characters with varying skills, knowledge, motivations, and desires come together to face some common threat, whether it's a dark overlord, a rampaging dragon, or a vizir putting suboptimal economic policies up for a vote in the king's counsel.

The difference between cooperation and collaboration is worth breaking down here. As the authors of *Therapeutically Applied Role-Playing Games: The Game To Grow Method* note, cooperative relationships are beneficial because they get people to help one another and share resources. *Collaborative* relationships, however, elevate interpersonal dynamics to another level because people build upon one another's contributions and capabilities to create something otherwise impossible.[9] These relationships make it possible to do something together that wouldn't be possible alone. This kind of collaboration is a critical life skill that predicts success in other spheres of life such as work[10] and education.[11] Game masters creating obstacles for their players should strive to find challenges that require all party members to contribute not only their mechanical abilities (class abilities, magic items, etc.) but also their unique role-playing skills, like character backstories, drives, and in-game relationships. Players should advocate for such opportunities and not overlook chances to participate, especially if this is a skill they're trying to develop.

TAKING OTHERS' PERSPECTIVES

As discussed extensively in Chapter 6, engaging in **perspective-taking** with other people and even fictional characters is a prerequisite for in-depth role-playing and is a skill that can be practiced through TTRPGs. This means not only being able to understand that others have their own minds, thoughts, feelings, desires, and experiences, but also being able to take all of that information into consideration when interacting with them.[12] This can help players get along with others by understanding their motivations.

Dungeons & Dragons encourages perspective-taking when players are asked to dream up backstories and personalities for their characters, which may or may not be drawn from their own lives. These backstories can be simple, or they can be elaborate tapestries of beliefs, biases, virtues, fears, morals, desires, worldviews, regrets, weaknesses, relationships, and hang-ups. Similarly, a given player is likely to learn other player characters' backstories and even those of some NPCs within the game world. In campaigns focused on role-play, anyone may be called upon to describe how their character thinks about or reacts to others given their knowledge of their character's perspective on the world.

This is a valuable skill to flex in other contexts besides TTRPGs. For people who struggle with anxiety over whether other people like them, developing perspective-taking can clarify that yes, they like you just fine; it's all this *other* stuff that has the person distracted or nonplussed. With that understanding in place, relationships are more likely to develop and flourish, people can trust each other more freely, and unproductive assumptions about others are more likely to drop away.

USING TTRPGS TO DEVELOP SKILLS IN THERAPEUTIC SETTINGS

In the last several years, *Dungeons & Dragons* has gained an interesting new audience: therapists and their clients. Role-play has a long history of use in therapy and it has even been used in group therapy settings. Going back to the 1930s, Romanian-American psychiatrist J. L. Moreno melded psychotherapy and improv theater in a practice he called psychodrama. According to a biography written by his son, Jonathan Moreno, the pioneering social scientist saw this as "an opportunity to get into action instead of just talking, to take the role of the important people in our lives to understand them better, to confront them imaginatively in the safety of the therapeutic theater, and most of all to become more creative and spontaneous human beings."[13] By the 1940s, other psychiatrists were citing Moreno's approach and the term "role-play" was coined.[14]

Today, many therapists swap out the theater angle to psychodrama but still hew close to the original idea of role-playing by using TTRPGs to promote mental health and help clients who need to develop mental or social skills. In her book, *Tabletop Role-Playing Therapy: A Guide for the Clinician Game Master*, therapist Dr. Megan Connell cites several reasons why games like *Dungeons & Dragons* are useful tools for therapy.[15] Perhaps the most basic is that playing these games can be a lot of fun, which motivates people to show up for and participate in therapy, which can be particularly challenging for children. They also tap into clients' special interests in genre entertainment such as fantasy or science fiction. Both of these can be true of any game or entertainment incorporated into therapy, but TTRPGs compound the effect by putting clients into groups and having them play together. This invokes not only shared goals and cooperation once players get comfortable with one another, but also creates shared experiences that can reinforce the lessons, insights, and reflections that the therapist provides. What's more, these experiences are much more flexible and malleable than other types of play, such as video games or board games. This flexibility allows the therapist to adapt to clients' specific needs.

This adaptability and flexibility are what Connell and others doing similar work note as the real strength of using TTRPGs in therapy. A game's characters, story, and rules allow therapeutic game masters to create bespoke situations that address treatment plans that they have created for their clients to help them reach their goals. Therapists exercise control over the game and the setting, consider the needs and diagnoses of the players, and plan to address them through the game. They may plan out or improvise encounters within the game that are tailored to help players safely deal with issues, practice skills, and learn from their experiences. Failing that, when things go sideways (as they often do), therapist game masters react to what their players are doing in the moment and make impromptu changes to the scenario to steer the play experience in beneficial directions when opportunities present themselves. And, unlike *Dungeons & Dragons* games outside of therapy, it's not uncommon for game masters to pause the game, ask players to step back and have a moment where everyone can debrief and reflect on what just happened and what it means for them. If, for example, a player who is working on her impulse control does something impetuous, the therapeutic game master might stop the action and ask the player if they can think of any other ways to react.

To this point, players who engage with TTRPGs in a therapy context often have specific issues, goals, and diagnoses that differ from most players you might meet down at the game shop or at a convention. They may be on the autism spectrum or they may have social anxiety, depression, attention deficit hyperactivity disorder, reading impairments, or posttraumatic stress disorder. As noted above, when working with such clients, therapeutic game masters develop specific plans, goals, and interventions. For someone anxious about doing or saying the wrong thing around others, for example, TTRPGs might be useful for the opportunities they present to make a social faux pas in a setting devoid of real-world consequences. Furthermore, the player can take advantage of the separation between themselves and their character to offload some of the anxiety—recall the concept of alibi from Chapter 7 that describes how players get to attribute their actions to role-playing a character. "In my groups," Dr. Megan Connell told me, "we pause quite often to process and talk. You might see therapeutic game masters rewinding time more and giving people do-overs, talking through emotions, and taking pauses to talk about how your character feels right now."[16] The group nature of the game also allows the therapist to facilitate discussions at the table about what other players are thinking or planning, which could be valuable information for an anxious client working to understand the otherwise unstated thoughts, reactions, and motivations of others so that they can better manage their thoughts.[17]

Upon reading all of this, you may be filled with aspirations to take a similar approach in your home *Dungeons & Dragons* games, which is understandable. Creating experiences custom-made to help your players grow, develop, and become mentally healthy is an admirable goal. Perhaps you see this as a way to further tailor the game to the needs and desires of your player. You should be careful, though, as caring for the mental well-being of other people in this way is something best left to qualified professionals. If you even have to ask yourself, "Am I a qualified professional?" then the answer is clearly, "No, you are not." People who are suited to provide for the mental health and well-being of other humans have dedicated years to the required education, licensure, and experience. This isn't to say that laypeople behind a game master screen can't strive to create meaningful, in-game experiences that stretch players and help them develop some of the skills discussed at the top of this chapter. But it's best not to try and help your players work through past trauma by recreating it in the game, throwing anxiety-producing situations at them, or pausing the game to talk about how they're not reading social situations correctly. Leave that to the professionals.

WHAT YOU LEARNED IN THIS CHAPTER

- TTRPGs frequently help players develop skills that are important in other parts of life, such as literacy, numeracy, logical reasoning, planning, communication, persuasion, cooperation, collaboration, perspective-taking, and more.
- The group nature and flexibility of TTRPGs also make them valuable tools for therapists looking to help clients with specific needs in a clinical context.

HOW TO APPLY THIS CHAPTER TO YOUR GAME

- As a game master, you can be attuned to the kinds of skills and experiences that the game puts in front of other players and tailor your game to meet their preferences.
- That said, leave probing and addressing mental health issues to the professionals.
- If you're not sure where the line between routine play and therapy is, err on the side of not engaging in therapy.
- When speaking to others outside of the game such as parents, school administrators, or others in need of convincing about the merits of TTRPGs, emphasize the social and skills-based nature of the game.

CONCLUSION

I hope I, along with the researchers I have cited, have convinced you that the study of human thoughts, emotions, and mental states is important to understanding the design and play of *Dungeons & Dragons* and other TTRPGs. And I hope that this helps you enjoy such games more and play on your terms. My goals were to teach you some interesting things about psychology and to provide you with some practical ways to apply the concepts to your own games, whether you're the game master or a player—and, of course, to tell some stories and make some jokes along the way.

That said, I do wish there had been more academic research to draw from. I frequently had to make inferential leaps using research from other contexts to generalize and apply the conclusions to TTRPGs and games in general. Given the long life of *Dungeons & Dragons* going back to the early 1970s, it's odd that there aren't more people out there spending their scholarly careers studying it. The game has existed longer than modern video games, for example, but the latter has been much more extensively studied. The reasons for that are debatable, but it's possible that TTRPGs are still seen as too niche of a hobby, or that the satanic panic of the 1980s left such a scar on the game that nobody is willing to fund serious research on it. Or it may be that doing controlled, scientific studies with tabletop games is too tricky given that it's a game played exclusively in small groups over long periods. That kind of thing doesn't scale well for most models of experimentation. It's too bad, but here's to hoping that some young researcher holding this book right now has become inspired to close that gap.

In that spirit, I have a companion website set up to keep the discussion of the psychology of games going after you have shelved this book or archived it in your electronic library. It's at www.psychologyofgames.com. There you can find many more articles and podcasts about the psychology of both tabletop role-playing games and video games. There were more interesting questions about the psychology of *Dungeons & Dragons* than I could fit in this book alone and explorations of those questions need a home somewhere. I hope to see you there!

GLOSSARY

Ability score – A character statistic that describes an innate ability relevant to gameplay mechanics. In *Dungeons & Dragons* these are Strength, Dexterity, Constitution, Intelligence, Wisdom, and Charisma.

Actual play – A type of media where people record themselves playing a tabletop role-playing game and make it available for streaming or downloading from the internet.

Armor class – A statistic from *Dungeons & Dragons* and some other games indicating how difficult it is to hit an enemy with an attack. Higher armor classes are harder to hit. Unless you're talking about the earliest editions of the game in which case lower numbers were harder to hit. Because *reasons*.

Bonus – See "Modifiers."

Campaign – A setting for an adventure or series of adventures. Also, the story told by the game in totality.

Character – See "Player Character (PC)."

Class – A specific job or role that characters fill. For example, wizard, fighter, or cleric in *Dungeons & Dragons*. Classes have different abilities, shortcomings, flavor, and responsibilities within the party.

Class ability – A special power available to a character because of their class or subclass.

Crit, critical hit – Rolling a 20 on a 20-sided die when attacking a foe. Exciting!

d20, d12, d10, d8, d6, d4 – Refers to a die and the number of faces it has. Players are often asked to "Roll a d20" which means to roll a 20-sided die. If they are asked to "roll two d6" it means to roll two six-sided dice.

Death save – A special die roll made to see whether a character dies or clings to life for another round when reduced to zero hit points.

Experience, experience points – One numerical way to gauge progress by characters in a TTRPG. Characters gain experience points by defeating monsters or accomplishing other in-game goals. They go up in levels at certain experience point thresholds.

Feat – A special power that characters can gain in the course of their career.

Game master or GM – The person who narrates the story, controls non-player characters/monsters and adjudicates the game rules. Among

Dungeons & Dragons players, the terms "dungeon master" or "DM" are often used and mean the same thing.

Game master screen – A reference tool consisting of a sturdy paper screen that game masters set up in front of themselves to prevent players from seeing their notes and dice rolls. Sometimes called a "dungeon master screen" by *Dungeons & Dragons* players.

Hit points – A numeric indicator of how close to death a character is. The fewer hit points, the worse shape they are in. Bad things happen when they are reduced to zero.

Homebrew – When the contents of a campaign or adventure are authored by the game master, even though it uses official rules for a game system. This is as opposed to an adventure or campaign setting published by Wizards of the Coast or another third-party author.

House rule – The addition of an unofficial rule or the omission of an official rule.

Initiative – A game mechanic used to determine what order participants in combat take their turns. Higher initiative numbers mean taking your turn earlier.

Inspiration point – A mechanic in *Dungeons & Dragons* where players are rewarded for good play with the one-time option to redo a bad d20 roll and thus improve their chances of success.

Level – A numerical measure of a character's power and/or experience. Characters go up in levels by gaining experience or progressing the game's story. They improve their abilities and statistics as they do so.

Live action role-play (LARP) – A type of game often inspired by but different from tabletop role-playing games. LARPers physically enact their characters' heroics with the aid of props, costumes, and real-world locations.

Metagaming – When a player applies or shares knowledge that their character should have no way of knowing.

Mini – Short for "miniature." A plastic or metal figure that represents a character or creature in the game. Typically used to aid in visualization of movement and position on a battle map. When used in a virtual table-top, minis are often called "tokens."

Modifiers – Numbers added to ("bonus") or subtracted from ("penalty") a die roll to determine the final outcome. Typically result from situational factors or ability scores.

Non-player character (NPC) – A character controlled by the game master instead of a player.

GLOSSARY

Party – A group of player characters. Like a murder of crows or a school of fish.

Penalty – See "Modifiers."

Player – Any person playing the game who is not the game master.

Player character (PC) – A character controlled by a player, as opposed to the game master.

Pregen – A character sheet that is pre-generated and ready to go for when a player wants to skip the character creation process.

Railroading – When the game master forces characters to make choices that fit a predetermined or desired sequence of events. As if the story were running on rails and can't deviate no matter what players do.

Role-playing – When a player acts and/or speaks as though they were their character. Game masters also frequently role-play non-player characters.

Rolling with advantage/disadvantage – Rolling a d20 twice and taking the better result (advantage) or the worse (disadvantage).

Safety tools – A system players and the game master agree upon for identifying and backing away from situations, topics, or other in-game content that is likely to cause distress or harm. For example, a card that any player can flash to pause the game and indicate that they are uncomfortable with the threat of child endangerment playing out in a scene.

Saving throw – A roll or "throw" of the die made in order to save a character from some bad effect. Saving throws are based on ability scores. For example, "Make a Wisdom saving throw."

Session – A length of time spent playing a tabletop role-playing game.

Session zero – A session that serves as a preamble to a new campaign where players and the game master take care of housekeeping, discuss house rules, familiarize themselves with the campaign setting, and set group norms.

Skill check – A roll of the die made to see if a character succeeds in some task related to a skill. For example, "Make an Athletics check."

Species – Called "race" in previous iterations of *Dungeons & Dragons*. Examples include human, elf, dwarf, or halfling.

Subclass – A specialization within a class that differentiates a character by giving them access to additional abilities.

Tabletop Role-playing game (TTRPG) – A collaborative, rules-based storytelling game where a group of players control characters.

Theater of the mind – A mode of play that eschews battle maps and miniatures in favor of asking everyone to imagine the scene and track things in their heads.

Virtual tabletop (VTT) – A computer program that recreates parts of the in-person role-playing game experience and otherwise lets people play through the internet.

Wizards of the Coast (WotC) – The current publishers of *Dungeons & Dragons*. They bought the property from the original publisher, TSR, in 1997.

REFERENCES

Aczel, A. (2005). *Chance: A guide to gambling, love, the stock market, and just about everything else.* Thunder Mouth Press.

Adam, H., & Galinsky, A. D. (2012). Enclothed cognition. *Journal of Experimental Social Psychology, 48*(4), 918–925. https://doi.org/10.1016/j.jesp.2012.02.008

Amsel, A. (1958). The role of frustrative non reward in non continuous reward situations. *Psychological Bulletin, 55*, 102–119. https://doi.org/10.1037/h0043125

Ariely, D. (2010). *The upside of irrationality: The unexpected benefits of defying logic at work and at home.* Harper Collins.

Aronson, E., & Mills, J. (1959). The effect of severity of initiation on liking for a group. *The Journal of Abnormal and Social Psychology, 59*(2), 177-181. https://doi.org/10.1037/h0047195

Au, A. K. C., & Chan, D. K. S. (2013). Organizational media choice in performance feedback: A multifaceted approach. *Journal of Applied Social Psychology, 43*(2), 397–407. https://doi.org/10.1111/j.1559-1816.2013.01009.x

Baard, P. P., Deci, E. L., & Ryan, R. M. (2004). Intrinsic need satisfaction: A motivational basis of performance and well-being in two work settings. *Journal of Applied Social Psychology, 34*(10), 2045-2068. https://doi.org/10.1111/j.1559-1816.2004.tb02690.x

Bailenson, J. N. (2021). Nonverbal overload: A theoretical argument for the causes of Zoom fatigue. *Technology, Mind, and Behavior, 2*(1). https://doi.org/10.1037/tmb0000030

Barsalou, L. W. (2008). Grounded cognition. *Annual Review of Psychology, 59*(1), 617–645. https://doi.org/10.1146/annurev.psych.59.103006.093639

Baumeister, R. F. (1991). *Escaping the self: Alcoholism, spirituality, masochism, and other flights from the burden of selfhood.* Basic Books.

Baumeister, R. F., & Leary, M. R. (1995). The need to belong: Desire for interpersonal attachments as a fundamental human motivation. *Psychological Bulletin, 117*(3), 497–529. https://doi.org/10.1037/0033-2909.117.3.497

Belk, R. W. (1988). Possessions and the extended self. *Journal of Consumer Research, 15*(September), 139–168. https://doi.org/10.1086/209154

Bennett, A. A., Campion, E. D., Keeler, K. R., & Keener, S. K. (2021). Videoconference fatigue? Exploring changes in fatigue after videoconference meetings during COVID-19. *Journal of Applied Psychology, 106*(3), 330–344. https://doi.org/10.1037/apl0000906

Bloom, P. (2010). "Irreplaceable," In *How pleasure works: the new science of why we like what we like* (pp. 91-115). W. W. Norton & Company.

Bowman, S. L., & Lieberoth, A. (2018). Psychology and role-playing games. In Zagal, J. P. & Deterding, S. (Eds.), *Role-playing game studies: Transmedia foundations* (pp. 245-264). Routledge.

Bowman, S. L., & Schrier, K. (2018). Players and their characters in RPGs. In Zagal, P. & Deterding, S. (Eds.), *Role-playing game studies: Transmedia foundations* (pp. 395–410). Routledge

Braga, J. P. N., Mata, A., Ferreira, M. B., & Sherman, S. J. (2017). Motivated reasoning in the prediction of sports outcomes and the belief in the "hot hand." *Cognition and Emotion, 31*(8), 1571–1580. https://doi.org/10.1080/02699931.2016.1244045

Brehm, J. (1966). *A Theory of psychological reactance.* Academic Press.

Broom, T. W., Chavez, R. S., & Wagner, D. D. (2021). Becoming the king in the north: Identification with fictional characters is associated with greater self–other neural overlap. *Social Cognitive and Affective Neuroscience, 16*(6), 541–551. https://doi.org/10.1093/scan/nsab021

Cannon-Bowers, J. A., Salas, E., & Converse, S. A. (1993). Shared mental models in expert team decision making. In Castellan, N. J. (Ed.), *Individual and group decision making: current issues* (pp. 221–246). Erlbaum. https://doi.org/10.1037/12169-019

Clark, L., Lawrence, A. J., Astley-Jones, F., & Gray, N. (2009). Gambling near-misses enhance motivation to gamble and recruit win-related brain circuitry. *Neuron, 61*(3), 481–490. https://doi.org/10.1016/j.neuron.2008.12.031

Coleman, J. S. (1988). Social capital in the creation of human capital. *American Journal of Sociology, 94,* 95–120. https://doi.org/10.1086/228943

Collins, E., & Cox, A. L. (2014). Switch on to games: Can digital games aid post-work recovery? *International Journal of Human-Computer Studies, 72*(8–9), 654–662. https://doi.org/10.1016/j.ijhcs.2013.12.006

Connell, M. (2023). *Tabletop role-playing therapy: A guide for the clinician game master.* W. W. Norton & Company.

Connell, M., Kilmer, E., & Kilmer, J. (2020). Tabletop role playing games in therapy. In Bean, A., Daniel, E., & Hays, S. (Eds.) *Integrating geek culture into therapeutic practice: The clinician's guide to geek therapy* (pp. 75-93). Leyline Publishing.

Cooper, W. H., Gallupe, R. B., Pollard, S., & Cadsby, J. (1998). Some liberating effects of anonymous electronic brainstorming. *Small Group Research, 29,* 147-78. https://psycnet.apa.org/doi/10.1177/1046496498292001

Davis, A., & Johns, A. (2020). Dungeons, dragons, and social development. In Bean, A., Daniel, E., & Hays, S. (Eds.) *Integrating geek culture into therapeutic practice: The clinician's guide to geek therapy* (pp. 95-107). Leyline Publishing.

Davis, M. H., Conklin, L., Smith, A., & Luce, C. (1996). Effect of perspective taking on the cognitive representation of persons: A merging of self and other. *Journal of Personality and Social Psychology, 70*(4), 713–726. https://doi.org/10.1037/0022-3514.70.4.713

Deci, E., & Ryan, R. M. (2000). The "what" and "why" of goal pursuits: Human needs and self-determination of behavior. *Psychological Inquiry, 11*(4), 227–268. https://doi.org/10.1207/S15327965PLI1104_01

Dixon, M. J., Harrigan, K. A., Sandhu, R., Collins, K., & Fugelsang, J. A. (2010). Losses disguised as wins in modern multi-line video slot machines. *Addiction, 105*(10), 1819–1824. https://doi.org/10.1111/j.1360-0443.2010.03050.x

Driskell, J. E., Salas, E., & Driskell, T. (2018). Foundations of teamwork and collaboration. American Psychologist, 73(4), 334–348. https://doi.org/10.1037/amp0000241

REFERENCES

Duncker, K. (1945). On problem-solving (L. S. Lees, Trans.). *Psychological Monographs*, 58(5), i–113. https://doi.org/10.1037/h0093599

Ehrhart, M. G., Schneider, B., & Macey, W. H. (2014). *Organizational climate and culture: An introduction to theory, research, and practice*. Routledge.

Engelstein, G. (2020). *Achievement relocked: Loss aversion and game design*. MIT Press. https://doi.org/10.7551/mitpress/12243.001.0001

Epley, N. (2008). Solving the (real) other minds problem: Mind reading. *Social and Personality Psychology Compass*, 2(3), 1455–1474. https://doi.org/10.1111/j.1751-9004.2008.00115.x

Fast, N. J., Gruenfeld, D. H., Sivanathan, N., & Galinsky, A. D. (2009). Illusory control. *Psychological Science*, 20(4), 502–508. https://doi.org/10.1111/j.1467-9280.2009.02311.x

Festinger, L. (1957). *A theory of cognitive dissonance (Vol. 2)*. Stanford University Press.

Fine, G. A. (1983). *Shared fantasy: Role-playing games as social worlds*. The University of Chicago Press.

Frank, M. G., & Gilovich, T. (1988). The dark side of self- and social perception: Black uniforms and aggression in professional sports. *Journal of Personality and Social Psychology*, 54(1), 74–85. https://doi.org/10.1037/0022-3514.54.1.74

Froming, W. J., Walker, G. R., & Lopyan, K.J. (1982). Public and private self-awareness: When personal attitudes conflict with societal expectations. *Journal of Experimental Social Psychology*, 18(5), 476-487. https://doi.org/10.1016/0022-1031(82)90067-1

Galston, W. A. (2000). Does the internet strengthen community? *National Civic Review*, 89(3), 193–202. https://doi.org/10.1002/ncr.89302

Giardina, A., Starcevic, V., King, D. L., Schimmenti, A., Di Blasi, M., & Billieux, J. (2021). Research directions in the study of gaming-related escapism: A commentary to Melodia, Canale, and Griffiths (2020). *International Journal of Mental Health and Addiction*, 12, 1075-1081. https://doi.org/10.1007/s11469-021-00642-8

Gilbert, D. T., & Ebert, J. E. J. (2002). Decisions and revisions: The affective forecasting of changeable outcomes. *Journal of Personality and Social Psychology*, 82(4), 503–514. https://doi.org/10.1037/0022-3514.82.4.503

Gilovich, T., Vallone, R., & Tversky, A. (1985). The hot hand in basketball: On the misperception of random sequences. *Cognitive Psychology*, 17(3), 295–314. https://doi.org/10.1016/0010-0285(85)90010-6

Graham, J., Nosek, B. A., Haidt, J., Iyer, R., Koleva, S., & Ditto, P. H. (2011). Mapping the moral domain. *Journal of Personality and Social Psychology*, 101(2), 366–385. https://doi.org/10.1037/a0021847

Grizzard, M., & Ahn, C. (2017). Morality & personality: Perfect & deviant selves. In Banks, J. (Ed.), *Avatar, assembled: The social and technical anatomy of digital bodies* (pp. 117-126). https://doi.org/10.3726/978-1-4331-3829-4

Haidt, J. (2001). The emotional dog and its rational tail: A social intuitionist approach to moral judgment. *Psychological Review*, 108(4), 814–834. https://doi.org/10.1037/0033-295X.108.4.814

Hedge, S. & Gouling, J. (Eds.), *Roleplaying games in the digital age: Essays on transmedia storytelling, tabletop RPGs and fandom* (235-252). McFarland & Company.

Henslin, J. (1967). Craps and magic. *American Journal of Sociology, 73*(3), 316–330. https://doi.org/10.1086/224479

Hsee, C. K., & Zhang, J. (2004). Distinction bias: Misprediction and mischoice due to joint evaluation. *Journal of Personality and Social Psychology, 86*(5), 680–695. https://doi.org/10.1037/0022-3514.86.5.680

Iyengar, S. (2010). *The art of choosing*. Twelve.

Iyengar, S. S., & Lepper, M. R. (2000). When choice is demotivating: Can one desire too much of a good thing? *Journal of Personality and Social Psychology, 79*(6), 995–1006. https://doi.org/10.1037//0022-3514.79.6.995

Iyengar, S. S., Wells, R. E., & Schwartz, B. (2006). Doing better but feeling worse: Looking for the "best" job undermines satisfaction. *Psychological Science, 17*(2), 143–150. https://doi.org/10.1111/j.1467-9280.2006.01677.x

Jerome, L. W., & Jordan, P. (2007). Psychophysiological perspective on presence: The implications of mediated environments on relationships, behavioral health and social construction. *Psychological Services 4*(2), 75–84. https://doi.org/10.1037/1541-1559.4.2.75

Joeckel, S., Bowman, N. D., & Dogruel, L. (2012). Gut or game? The influence of moral intuitions on decisions in video games. *Media Psychology, 15*(4), 460–485. https://doi.org/10.1080/15213269.2012.727218

Johnson, R. E., Chang, C., & Lord, R. G. (2006). Moving from cognition to behavior: What the research says. *Psychological Bulletin, 132*, 381– 415. https://doi.org/10.1037/0033-2909.132.3.381

Jostman, N. B., Lakens, D., & Schubert, T. W. (2009). Weight as an embodiment of importance. *Psychological Science, 20*, 1169–1174. https://doi.org/10.1111/j.1467-9280.2009.02426.x

Kaufman, G. F., & Libby, L. K. (2012). Changing beliefs and behavior through experience-taking. *Journal of Personality and Social Psychology, 103*(1), 1–19. https://doi.org/10.1037/a0027525"

Kaufman, G. F., & Libby, L. K. (2012). Changing beliefs and behavior through experience-taking. *Journal of Personality and Social Psychology, 103*(1), 1–19. https://doi.org/10.1037/a0027525

Kaylor, S. L. B. (2017). Dungeons and Dragons and literacy: The role tabletop role-playing games can play in developing teenagers' literacy skills and reading interests. *Graduate Research Papers, 215*. https://scholarworks.uni.edu/grp/215

Kilmer. E., Adam, D., Kilmer, J., & Johns, A. (2023). Case conceptualization and treatment planning in therapeutically applied role-playing games. In Kilmer. E., Adam, D. Kilmer, J. & Johns, A. (Eds.) *Therapeutically applied role-playing games: The Game To Grow method* (pp. 113-142). Routledge.

Kilmer. E., Adam, D., Kilmer, J., & Johns, A. (Eds.) *Therapeutically applied role-playing games: The Game To Grow method* (pp. 113-142). Routledge.

Klimmt, C., & Vorderer, P. (2003). Media psychology 'Is not yet there': Introducing theories on media entertainment to the presence debate.

REFERENCES

Presence: Teleoperators and Virtual Environments 12(4), 346–59. https://doi.org/10.1162/105474603322391596

Kohn, N. W., Paulus, P. B., & Choi, Y. (2011). Building on the ideas of others: An examination of the idea combination process. *Journal of Experimental Social Psychology, 47*(3), 554–561. https://doi.org/10.1016/j.jesp.2011.01.004

Kowert R., Oldmeadow J.A. (2013). (A)social reputation: Exploring the relationship between online video game involvement and social competence. *Computers In Human Behavior, 29*(4), 1872–1878. doi:10.1016/j.chb.2010.07.015

Kowert, R & Quandt, T. (Eds.), *The Routledge handbook of digital media and communication* (pp. 87-98). Routledge.

Kubey, R. W., & Csikszentmihalyi, M. (1990). Television as escape: Subjective experience before an evening of heavy viewing. *Communication Reports, 3*(2), 92–100. https://doi.org/10.1080/08934219009367509

Kuss, D. J. (2013). Internet gaming addiction: Current perspectives. *Psychology Research and Behavior Management, 6*, 125–137. https://doi.org/10.2147/prbm.s39476

Laal, M., Naseri, A. S., Laal, M., & Khattami-Kermanshahi, Z. (2013). What do we achieve from learning in collaboration? *Procedia - Social and Behavioral Sciences, 93*, 1427–1432. https://doi.org/10.1016/j.sbspro.2013.10.057

Ladoucer, R., Paquet, C., & Dube, D. (1996). Erroneous perceptions in generating sequences of random events. *Journal of Applied Social Psychology, 2*(26), 2157–2166. https://doi.org/10.1111/j.1559-1816.1996.tb01793.x

Lankoski, P., & Järvelä, S. (2012). An Embodied cognition approach for understanding role-playing. *International Journal of Role-Playing, 3*, 18–32. http://dx.doi.org/10.33063/ijrp.vi3.222

Leonard, D. J., & College, C. (2015). Bleed-out on the brain: The neuroscience of character-to-player spillover in larp. *International Journal of Role-Playing, 9*, 9–15. https://doi.org/10.33063/ijrp.vi9.266

Lillard, A. S. (1993). Pretend play skills and the child's theory of mind. *Child Development, 64*(2), 348. https://doi.org/10.2307/1131255

Lim, B.-C., & Klein, K. J. (2006). Team mental models and team performance: A field study of the effects of team mental model similarity and accuracy. *Journal of Organizational Behavior, 27*(4), 403–418. https://doi.org/10.1002/job.387

Liu, W., & Gal, D. (2011). Bringing us together or driving us apart: The effect of soliciting consumer input on consumers' propensity to transact with an organization. *Journal of Consumer Research, 38*(2), 242–259. https://doi.org/10.1086/658884

Lombard, M., & Ditton, T. (1997). At the heart of it all: The concept of presence. *Journal of Computer-Mediated Communication, 3*(2). https://doi.org/10.1111/j.1083-6101.1997.tb00072.x

Mardon, R., & Belk, R. (2018). Materializing digital collecting: An extended view of digital materiality. *Marketing Theory*. https://doi.org/10.1177/1470593118767725

Marsh, L. E., Kanngiesser, P., & Hood, B. (2018). When and how does labour lead to love? The ontogeny and mechanisms of the IKEA effect. *Cognition, 170*, 245-253. https://doi.org/10.1016/j.cognition.2017.10.012

Marzis, M. (1975). Antipollution measures and psychological reactance theory: A field experiment. *Journal of Personality and Social Psychology 31*(4). https://doi.org/10.1037/h0077075

Mathieu, J. E., Heffner, T. S., Goodwin, G. F., Hobson, K., Ivory, K., Trip, M., & Windefelder, N. (2000). The influence of shared mental models on team process and performance. *Journal of Applied Psychology, 85*(2), 273–283. https://doi.org/10.1287/mnsc.1040.0210

Mehrabian, A. (1969). Some referents and measures of nonverbal behavior. *Behavioral Research Methods & Instruments, 1*(6), 203–207. https://psycnet.apa.org/doi/10.3758/BF03208096

Meriläinen, M. (2011). The self-perceived effects of the role-playing hobby on personal development -- A survey report. *International Journal of Role Playing, 3*, 49–68. https://doi.org/10.33063/ijrp.vi3.224

Miron, A., & Brehm, J. (2006). Reactance theory - 40 years later. *Zeitschrift Für Sozialpsychologie, 37*(1), 3–12. https://doi.org/10.1024/0044-3514.37.1.9

Mochon, D., Norton, M. I., & Ariely, D. (2012). Bolstering and restoring feelings of competence via the IKEA effect. *International Journal of Research in Marketing, 29*(4), 363–369. https://doi.org/10.1016/j.ijresmar.2012.05.001

Moreno, J. D. (2014). *Impromptu man: J. L. Moreno and the origins of psychodrama, encounter culture, and the social network*. Bellevue Literary Press.

Nemeth, C. J., & Ormiston, M. (2007). Creative idea generation: Harmony versus stimulation. *European Journal of Social Psychology, 37*(3), 524–535. https://doi.org/10.1002/ejsp.373

Nemeth, C. J., Personnaz, B., Personnaz, M., & Goncalo, J. A. (2004). The liberating role of conflict in group creativity: A study in two countries. *European Journal of Social Psychology, 34*(4), 365–374. https://doi.org/10.1002/ejsp.210

Newman, G. E., Diesendruck, G., & Bloom, P. (2011). Celebrity contagion and the value of objects. *Journal of Consumer Research, 38*(2), 215–228. https://doi.org/10.1086/658999

Niedenthal, P. M., Barsalou, L. W., Winkielman, P., Krauth-Gruber, S., & Ric, F. (2005). Embodiment in attitudes, social perception, and emotion. *Personality and Social Psychology Review, 9*(3), 184–211. https://doi.org/10.1207/s15327957pspr0903_1

Nijstad, B. A., & Stroebe, W. (2006). How the group affects the mind: A cognitive model of idea generation in groups. *Personality and Social Psychology Review, 10*(3), 186–213. https://doi.org/10.1207/s15327957pspr1003_1

Norton, M., Mochon, D., & Ariely, D. (2012). The "IKEA effect": When labor leads to love. *Journal of Consumer Psychology, 22*(3), 453–460. https://psycnet.apa.org/doi/10.1016/j.jcps.2011.08.002

Oatley, K. (1994). A taxonomy of the emotions of literary response and a theory of identification in fictional narrative. *Poetics, 23*, 53–74. https://doi.org/10.1016/0304-422X(94)P4296-S

Osborn, A. F. (1957). *Applied imagination: Principles and procedures of creative problem solving*. Scribner.

REFERENCES

Oskarsson, A. T., Van Boven, L., McClelland, G. H., & Hastie, R. (2009). What's next? Judging sequences of binary events. *Psychological Bulletin, 135*(2), 262–285. https://doi.org/10.1037/a0014821

Parke, J., & Griffiths, M. (2004). Gambling addiction and the evolution of the "near miss." *Addiction Research and Theory, 12*(5), 407–411. https://doi.org/10.1080/16 066350410001728118

Paulus, P. B. & Nijstad. B. A. (Eds.) *Handbook of group creativity and innovation.* Oxford University Press.

Paulus, P. B., Putman, V. L., Dugosh, K. L., Dzindolet, M. T., & Coskun, H. (2002). Social and cognitive influences in group brainstorming: Predicting production gains and losses. *European Review of Social Psychology, 12*(1), 299–325. https://doi.org/10.1080/14792772143000094

Peck, J., & Shu, S. B. (2009). The effect of mere touch on perceived ownership. *Journal of Consumer Research, 36*(3), 434-47. https://doi.org/10.1086/598614

Peterson, J. (2020). *The elusive shift: How role-playing games forged their identity.* MIT Press.

Putnam R. (2000). *Bowling alone: The collapse and revival of American community.* Simon & Schuster.

Ratan, R., Miller, D. B., & Bailenson, J. N. (2022). Facial Appearance Dissatisfaction Explains Differences in Zoom Fatigue. *Cyberpsychology, Behavior, and Social Networking, 25*(2), 124–129. https://doi.org/10.1089/cyber.2021.0112

Rauscher, F. H., Krauss, R. M., & Chen, Y. (1996). Gesture, speech, and lexical access: The role of lexical movements in speech production. *Psychological Science, 7,* 226-231. https://doi.org/10.1111/j.1467-9280.1996.tb00364.x

Reinecke, L. (2009). Games and recovery: The use of video and computer games to recuperate from stress and strain. *Journal of Media Psychology, 21*(3), 126–142. https://doi.org/10.1027/1864-1105.21.3.126

Rigby, S. C., & Ryan, R. M. (2011). *Glued to games: How video games draw us in and hold us spellbound.* Praeger.

Rouse, W. B., & Morris, N. M. (1986). On looking into the black box: Prospects and limits in the search for mental models. *Psychological Bulletin, 100,* 349 –363. https://psycnet.apa.org/doi/10.1037/0033-2909.100.3.349

Ryan, R. M., Bernstein, J. H., & Brown, K. W. (2010). Weekends, work, and well-being: Psychological need satisfactions and day of the week effects on mood, vitality, and physical symptoms. *Journal of Social and Clinical Psychology, 29*(1), 95–122. https://doi.org/10.1521/jscp.2010.29.1.95

Ryan, R. M., Rigby, S. C., & Przybylski, A. K. (2006). The motivational pull of video games: A self-determination heory approach. *Motivation and Emotion, 30*(4), 344–360. https://doi.org/10.1007/s11031-006-9051-8

Schneider, B., Ehrhart, M. G., & Macey, W. (2013). Organizational climate and culture. *Annual Review of Psychology* 64. https://doi.org/10.1146/annurev-psych-113011-143809

Schwartz, B., Ward, A., Monterosso, J., Lyubomirsky, S., White, K., & Lehman, D. R. (2002). Maximizing versus satisficing: Happiness is a matter of choice. *Journal of Personality and Social Psychology, 83*(5), 1178–1197. https://doi.org/10.1037/0022-3514.83.5.1178

Scriven, P. (2021). From tabletop to screen: Playing Dungeons and Dragons during COVID-19. *Societies, 11*(4), 125 https://doi.org/10.3390/soc11040125

Simon, H. A. (1955). A behavioral model of rational choice. *Quarterly Journal of Economics, 59*, 99-118. https://doi.org/10.2307/1884852

Skinner, B. F. (1992). "Superstition" in the pigeon. 1948. *Journal of Experimental Psychology. General, 121*(3), 273–274. https://doi.org/10.1037/0096-3445.121.3.273

Sleiman, A. A., Sigurjonsdottir, S., Elnes, A., Gage, N. A., & Gravina, N. E. (2020). A quantitative review of performance feedback in organizational settings (1998-2018). *Journal of Organizational Behavior Management, 40*(3-4), 303-332. https://doi.org/10.1080/01608061.2020.1823300

Sonnentag, S., & Bayer, U.V. (2005). Switching off mentally: Predictors and consequences of psychological detachment from work during off-job time. *Journal of Occupational Health Psychology, 10*(4), 393–414. https://doi.org/10.1037/1076-8998.10.4.393

Sonnentag, S., & Zijlstra, F. R. H. (2006). Job characteristics and off-job activities as predictors of need for recovery, well-being, and fatigue. *Journal Of Applied Psychology, 91*(2). https://psycnet.apa.org/doi/10.1037/0021-9010.91.2.330

Stenseng, F., Falch-Madsen, J., & Hygen, B. W. (2021). Are there two types of escapism? Exploring a dualistic model of escapism in digital gaming and online streaming. *Psychology of Popular Media, 10*(3), 319–329. https://doi.org/10.1037/ppm0000339

Stenseng, F., Rise, J., & Kraft, P. (2012). Activity engagement as escape from self: The role of self-suppression and self-expansion. *Leisure Sciences, 34*(1), 19–38. https://doi.org/10.1080/01490400.2012.633849

Strack, F., Martin, L. L., & Stepper, S. (1988). Inhibiting and facilitating conditions of the human smile: A nonobtrusive test of the facial feedback hypothesis. *Journal of Personality and Social Psychology, 54*(5), 768–777. https://doi.org/10.1037/0022-3514.54.5.768

Strickland, L. H, & Grote, F. W. (1967). Temporal presentation of winning symbols and slot machine playing. *Journal of Experimental Psychology, 74*(1), 10–13. https://doi.org/10.1037/h0024511

Tamborini, R., Bowman, N. D., Prabhu, S., Hahn, L., Klebig, B., Grall, C., & Novotny, E. (2018). The effect of moral intuitions on decisions in video game play: The impact of chronic and temporary intuition accessibility. *New Media and Society, 20*(2), 564–580. https://doi.org/10.1177/1461444816664356

Taylor, D. W., Berry, P. C., & Block, C. H. (1958). Does group participation when using brainstorming facilitate or inhibit creative thinking? *Administrative Science Quarterly, 3*, 23-47. https://psycnet.apa.org/doi/10.2307/2390603

Tomprou, M., Kim, Y. J., Chikersal, P., Woolley, A. W., & Dabbish, L. A. (2021). Speaking out of turn: How video conferencing reduces vocal synchrony and collective intelligence. *PLOS ONE, 16*(3), e0247655. https://doi.org/10.1371/journal.pone.0247655

Trepte, S., Reinecke, L., & Juechems, K. (2012). The social side of gaming: How playing online computer games creates online and offline social support. *Computers in Human Behavior, 28*(3), 832–839. https://doi.org/10.1016/j.chb.2011.12.003

REFERENCES

Tversky, A. (1972). Elimination by aspects: A theory of choice. *Psychological Review, 79*(4), 281–299. https://doi.org/10.1037/h0032955

Valkenburg, P. M., & Peter, J. (2009). Social consequences of the internet for adolescents: A decade of research. *Current Directions in Psychological Science, 18*(1), 1-5. https://doi.org/10.1111/j.1467-8721.2009.01595.x

Waller, M. J., Gupta, N., & Giambatista, R. C. (2004). Effects of adaptive behaviors and shared mental models on control crew performance. *Management Science, 50*(11), 1534–1544. https://doi.org/10.1287/mnsc.1040.0210

Wells, G. L., & Petty, R. E. (1980). The effects of overt head movements on persuasion: Compatibility and incompatibility of responses. *Basic and Applied Social Psychology, 1*, 219-230. https://doi.org/10.1207/s15324834basp0103_2

Williams, D. (2007). The Impact of time online: Social capital and cyberbalkanization. *CyberPsychology & Behavior, 10*(3), 398–406. https://doi.org/10.1089/cpb.2006.9939

Williams, L. E., & Bargh, J. A. (2008). Experiencing physical warmth promotes interpersonal warmth. *Science, 322*, 606–607. https://doi.org/10.1126/science.1162548

Wilson, T. D., & Schooler, J. W. (1991). Thinking Too Much: Introspection can reduce the quality of preferences and decisions. *Journal of Personality and Social Psychology, 60*(2), 181–192. https://doi.org//0022-3514.60.2.181

Wilson, T. D., Lisle, D. J., Schooler, J. W., Hodges, S. D., Klaaren, K. J., & LaFleur, S. J. (1993). Introspecting about reasons can reduce post-choice satisfaction. *Personality and Social Psychology Bulletin, 19*(3), 331–339. https://doi.org/10.1177/0146167293193010

Wirth, W., Hartmann, T., Böcking, S., Vorderer, P., Klimmt, C., Schramm, H., Saari, T., Laarni, J., Ravaja, N., Gouveia, F. R., Biocca, F., Sacau, A., Jäncke, L., Baumgartner, T., & Jäncke, P. (2007). A process model of the formation of spatial presence experiences. *Media Psychology, 9*(3), 493–525. https://doi.org/10.1080/15213260701283079

Wirth, W., Hofer, M., & Schramm, H. (2012). The Role of emotional involvement and trait absorption in the formation of spatial presence. *Media Psychology, 15*(1), 19–43. https://doi.org/10.1080/15213269.2011.648536

Wirth, W., Ryffel, F., von Pape, T., & Karnowski, V. (2013). The development of video game enjoyment in a role playing game. *Cyberpsychology, Behavior and Social Networking, 16*(4), 260–264. https://doi.org/10.1089/cyber.2012.0159

Worchel, S., Lee, J., & Adewole, A. (1975). Effects of supply and demand on ratings of object value. *Journal of Personality and Social Psychology, 32*(5), 906–914. https://doi.org/10.1037/0022-3514.32.5.906

Yee, N. (2013). *The Proteus paradox: How online games and virtual worlds change us-and how they don't*. Yale University Press.

Zagal, J. P. & Deterding, S. (Eds.), *Role-playing game studies: Transmedia foundations* (pp. 395-410). Routledge.

ENDNOTES

Chapter 1:

1 These and other quotes here come from direct personal correspondences with the author.

2 Deci, E., & Ryan, R. M. (2000). The "what" and "why" of goal pursuits: Human needs and self-determination of behavior. *Psychological Inquiry, 11*(4), 227–268. https://doi.org/10.1207/S15327965PLI1104_01

3 Ryan, R. M., Rigby, S. C., & Przybylski, A. K. (2006). The motivational pull of video games: A self-determination heory approach. *Motivation and Emotion, 30*(4), 344–360. https://doi.org/10.1007/s11031-006-9051-8

4 Engelstein, G. (2020). *Achievement relocked: Loss aversion and game design.* MIT Press. https://doi.org/10.7551/mitpress/12243.001.0001

5 Rigby, S. C., & Ryan, R. M. (2011). Games and the need for competence. In *glued to games: How video games draw us in and hold us spellbound* (page 15). Praeger.

6 Gygax, G. (1979). *Advanced dungeons and dragons monster manual.* TSR Hobbies.

7 Ibid., page 100.

8 Englestein, *Achievement relocked,* page 12.

9 See https://somethingpositive.net/comic/peejee-dragons-pt-6/

10 Shae, M. (2022, March 21). *Lightning rods – showcase powerful character abilities.* SlyFlourish.com. Retrieved July 2, 2022, from https://slyflourish.com/lightning_rods.html

11 Di, G. (2022, February 16). The underused DM tip that will make players obsessed with your game. [Video]. YouTube. https://youtu.be/Bd6xX3i7Qeo

12 Dixon, M. J., Harrigan, K. A., Sandhu, R., Collins, K., & Fugelsang, J. A. (2010). Losses disguised as wins in modern multi-line video slot machines. *Addiction, 105*(10), 1819–1824. https://doi.org/10.1111/j.1360-0443.2010.03050.x

Chapter 2:

1 I really doubt he'll read this, but it would be AMAZING if he did.

2 Fine, G. A. (1983). *Role-playing games as social worlds.* The University of Chicago Press.

3 Baard, P. P., Deci, E. L., & Ryan, R. M. (2004). Intrinsic need satisfaction: A motivational basis of performance and well-being in two work settings. *Journal of Applied Social Psychology, 34*(10), 2045-2068. https://doi.org/10.1111/j.1559-1816.2004.tb02690.x

4 Ryan, R. M., Bernstein, J. H., & Brown, K. W. (2010). Weekends, work, and well-being: Psychological need satisfactions and day of the week effects on mood, vitality, and physical symptoms. *Journal of Social and Clinical Psychology, 29*(1), 95–122. https://doi.org/10.1521/jscp.2010.29.1.95

5 Dungeon Craft (2021, December 28). The problem with leveling up in Dungeons & Dragons. YouTube. https://youtu.be/2mcCBdXe1Vg

6 Brehm, J. (1966). *A Theory of psychological reactance.* Academic Press.

7 For more on psychological reactance, see Miron, A., & Brehm, J. (2006). Reactance theory - 40 years later. *Zeitschrift Für Sozialpsychologie, 37*(1), 3–12. https://doi.org/10.1024/0044-3514.37.1.9

8 Marzis, M. (1975). Antipollution measures and psychological reactance theory: A field experiment. *Journal of Personality and Social Psychology 31*(4). https://doi.org/10.1037/h0077075

9 No, Kevin, I'm not letting this go.

10 Anonymous (1985, April). Nogard. *Dragon, 9*(3), 43-45.

Chapter 3:

1 Meriläinen, M. (2011). The self-perceived effects of the role-playing hobby on personal development – A survey report. *International Journal of Role Playing, 3*, 49–68. https://doi.org/10.33063/ijrp.vi3.224

2 For example, see Baumeister, R. F., & Leary, M. R. (1995). The need to belong: Desire for interpersonal attachments as a fundamental human motivation. *Psychological Bulletin, 117*(3), 497–529. https://doi.org/10.1037/0033-2909.117.3.497

3 Ryan, R. M., Rigby, S. C., & Przybylski, A. K. (2006). The motivational pull of video games: A self-determination theory approach. *Motivation and Emotion, 30*(4), 344–360. https://doi.org/10.1007/s11031-006-9051-8

4 Rigby, S. C., & Ryan, R. M. (2011). *Glued to games: How video games draw us in and hold Us spellbound.* Praeger.

5 ...Yet.

6 Sleiman, A. A., Sigurjonsdottir, S., Elnes, A., Gage, N. A., & Gravina, N. E. (2020). A quantitative review of performance feedback in organizational settings (1998-2018). *Journal of Organizational Behavior Management, 40*(3–4), 303–332. https://doi.org/10.1080/01608061.2020.1823300

7 Johnson, R. E., Chang, C., & Lord, R. G. (2006). Moving from cognition to behavior: What the research says. *Psychological Bulletin, 132*, 381– 415. https://doi.org/10.1037/0033-2909.132.3.381

8 Au, A. K. C., & Chan, D. K. S. (2013). Organizational media choice in performance feedback: A multifaceted approach. *Journal of Applied Social Psychology, 43*(2), 397–407. https://doi.org/10.1111/j.1559-1816.2013.01009.x

Chapter 4:

1 Originally published in 1981 and written by Dave J. Brown along with Don Turnbull, the version of this adventure I played appeared in 2019's *Ghosts of Saltmarsh* by Wizards of the Coast.

2 Wirth, W., Ryffel, F., von Pape, T., & Karnowski, V. (2013). The development of video game enjoyment in a role playing game. *Cyberpsychology, Behavior and Social Networking, 16*(4), 260–264. https://doi.org/10.1089/cyber.2012.0159

3 Wirth, W., Hofer, M., & Schramm, H. (2012). The Role of emotional involvement and trait absorption in the formation of spatial presence. *Media Psychology, 15*(1), 19–43. https://doi.org/10.1080/15213269.2011.648536

ENDNOTES

4 Klimmt, C., & Vorderer, P. (2003). Media psychology 'Is not yet there': Introducing theories on media entertainment to the presence debate. *Presence: Teleoperators and Virtual Environments 12*(4), 346–59. https://doi.org/10.1162/105474603322391596

5 Wirth, W., Hartmann, T., Böcking, S., Vorderer, P., Klimmt, C., Schramm, H., Saari, T., Laarni, J., Ravaja, N., Gouveia, F. R., Biocca, F., Sacau, A., Jäncke, L., Baumgartner, T., & Jäncke, P. (2007). A process model of the formation of spatial presence experiences. *Media Psychology, 9*(3), 493–525. https://doi.org/10.1080/15213260701283079

6 Ibid.

7 Jerome, L. W., & Jordan, P. (2007). Psychophysiological perspective on presence: The implications of mediated environments on relationships, behavioral health and social construction. *Psychological Services 4*(2), 75–84. https://doi.org/10.1037/1541-1559.4.2.75

8 Lombard, M., & Ditton, T. (1997). At the heart of it all: The concept of presence. *Journal of Computer-Mediated Communication, 3*(2). https://doi.org/10.1111/j.1083-6101.1997.tb00072.x

9 Wirth et al. "A process model for the formation of spatial presence."

10 Ibid.

11 Oatley, K. (1994). A taxonomy of the emotions of literary response and a theory of identification in fictional narrative. *Poetics, 23*, 53–74. https://doi.org/10.1016/0304-422X(94)P4296-S

12 Lombard & Ditton "At the heart of it all."

13 Klimmt & Vorderer, "Media psychology 'Is not yet there.'"

14 Wirth, Hofer, & Schramm "The role of emotional involvement."

15 Ibid., page 29.

16 Wirth et al. "A process model for the formation of spatial presence."

Chapter 5:

1 Things get muddy since Wizards of the Coast bought TSR in 1997 and continued publishing things under the TSR banner for a while. The point is that Kammer's collection is extensive and comprehensive.

2 This and other quotes attributed to Alex Kammer were taken from a personal correspondence between Kammer and the author on December 8, 2022.

3 See https://www.enworld.org/threads/the-making-and-breaking-of-deities-demigods.666377/

4 Worchel, S., Lee, J., & Adewole, A. (1975). Effects of supply and demand on ratings of object value. *Journal of Personality and Social Psychology, 32*(5), 906–914. https://doi.org/10.1037/0022-3514.32.5.906

5 That was it. That was my one "eye of the beholder" joke the contract with my publisher allows me to make in this entire book. SORRY NOT SORRY.

6 Belk, R. W. (1988). Possessions and the extended self. *Journal of Consumer Research, 15*(September), 139–168. https://doi.org/10.1086/209154

7 Mardon, R., & Belk, R. (2018). Materializing digital collecting: An extended view of digital materiality. *Marketing Theory*. https://doi.org/10.1177/1470593118767725

8 Bloom, P. (2010). "Irreplaceable," In *How pleasure works: the new science of why we like what we like* (pp. 91-115). W. W. Norton & Company.

9 Newman, G. E., Diesendruck, G., & Bloom, P. (2011). Celebrity contagion and the value of objects. *Journal of Consumer Research, 38*(2), 215–228. https://doi.org/10.1086/658999

10 Belk, R. W. (1988). Possessions and the extended self. *Journal of Consumer Research*, 15(September), 139–168. https://doi.org/10.1086/209154

Chapter 6:

1 Peterson, J. (2012). System - The rules of the game. In *Playing at the world: A history of simulating wars, people, and fantastic adventures from chess to role-playing games*. Unreason Press.

2 Ibid.

3 Peterson, J. (2020). The two cultures. In *the elusive shift - How role-playing games forged their identity* (pp. 1-35). MIT Press.

4 Ibid.

5 Peterson, Playing at the world.

6 Meriläinen, M. (2011). The self-perceived effects of the role-playing hobby on personal development – A survey report. *International Journal of Role Playing, 3*, 49–68. https://doi.org/10.33063/ijrp.vi3.224

7 Davis, M. H., Conklin, L., Smith, A., & Luce, C. (1996). Effect of perspective taking on the cognitive representation of persons: A merging of self and other. *Journal of Personality and Social Psychology, 70*(4), 713–726. https://doi.org/10.1037/0022-3514.70.4.713

8 Epley, N. (2008). Solving the (real) other minds problem: Mind reading. *Social and Personality Psychology Compass, 2*(3), 1455–1474. https://doi.org/10.1111/j.1751-9004.2008.00115.x

9 Ibid.

10 Broom, T. W., Chavez, R. S., & Wagner, D. D. (2021). Becoming the king in the north: Identification with fictional characters is associated with greater self–other neural overlap. *Social Cognitive and Affective Neuroscience, 16*(6), 541–551. https://doi.org/10.1093/scan/nsab021

11 Kaufman, G. F., & Libby, L. K. (2012). Changing beliefs and behavior through experience-taking. *Journal of Personality and Social Psychology, 103*(1), 1–19. https://doi.org/10.1037/a0027525"

12 Fine, G. A. (1983). *Shared fantasy: Role-playing games as social worlds*. The University of Chicago Press.

13 Connell, M. (2023). *Role-playing therapy: A guide for the clinician game master*. Norton.

14 Kaufman, G. F., & Libby, L. K. (2012). Changing beliefs and behavior through experience-taking. *Journal of Personality and Social Psychology, 103*(1), 1–19. https://doi.org/10.1037/a0027525

ENDNOTES

15 Bowman, S. L., & Lieberoth, A. (2018). Psychology and role-playing games. In Zagal, J. P. & Deterding, S. (Eds.), *Role-playing game studies: Transmedia foundations* (pp. 245-264). Routledge.

16 Leonard, D. J., & College, C. (2015). Bleed-out on the brain: The neuroscience of character-to-player spillover in larp. *International Journal of Role-Playing, 9*, 9–15. https://doi.org/10.33063/ijrp.vi9.266

17 Bowman & Schrier, Players and their characters in RPGs.

Chapter 7:

1 Lillard, A. S. (1993). Pretend play skills and the child's theory of mind. *Child Development, 64*(2), 348. https://doi.org/10.2307/1131255

2 Ibid.

3 Well, technically organizational psychologists call the concept "organizational climate" BUT I DON'T CARE because everyone else calls it "culture" so we're going with that and this footnote is my defense against the pedants.

4 Schneider, B., Ehrhart, M. G., & Macey, W. (2013). Organizational climate and culture. *Annual Review of Psychology 64*. https://doi.org/10.1146/annurev-psych-113011-143809

5 Ehrhart, M. G., Schneider, B., & Macey, W. H. (2014). *Organizational climate and culture: An introduction to theory, research, and practice.* Routledge.

6 Bowman, S. L. & Schrier, K. (2018). Players and their characters in role-playing games. In Zagal, J. P. & Deterding, S. (Eds.), *Role-playing game studies: Transmedia foundations* (pp. 395-410). Routledge.

7 Barsalou, L. W. (2008). Grounded cognition. *Annual Review of Psychology, 59*(1), 617–645. https://doi.org/10.1146/annurev.psych.59.103006.093639

8 Hat tip for this example to Niedenthal, P. M., Barsalou, L. W., Winkielman, P., Krauth-Gruber, S., & Ric, F. (2005). Embodiment in attitudes, social perception, and emotion. *Personality and Social Psychology Review, 9*(3), 184–211. https://doi.org/10.1207/s15327957pspr0903_1

9 Wells, G. L., & Petty, R. E. (1980). The effects of overt head movements on persuasion: Compatibility and incompatibility of responses. *Basic and Applied Social Psychology, 1*, 219-230. https://doi.org/10.1207/s15324834basp0103_2

10 Strack, F., Martin, L. L., & Stepper, S. (1988). Inhibiting and facilitating conditions of the human smile: A nonobtrusive test of the facial feedback hypothesis. *Journal of Personality and Social Psychology, 54*(5), 768–777. https://doi.org/10.1037/0022-3514.54.5.768

11 Williams, L. E., & Bargh, J. A. (2008). Experiencing physical warmth promotes interpersonal warmth. *Science, 322*, 606–607. https://doi.org/10.1126/science.1162548

12 Jostman, N. B., Lakens, D., & Schubert, T. W. (2009). Weight as an embodiment of importance. *Psychological Science, 20*, 1169–1174. https://doi.org/10.1111/j.1467-9280.2009.02426.x

13 Rauscher, F. H., Krauss, R. M., & Chen, Y. (1996). Gesture, speech, and lexical access: The role of lexical movements in speech production. *Psychological Science, 7*, 226-231. https://doi.org/10.1111/j.1467-9280.1996.tb00364.x

14 Ibid.

15 Lankoski, P., & Järvelä, S. (2012). An Embodied cognition approach for understanding role-playing. *International Journal of Role-Playing, 3*, 18–32. http://dx.doi.org/10.33063/ijrp.vi3.222

16 Adam, H., & Galinsky, A. D. (2012). Enclothed cognition. *Journal of Experimental Social Psychology, 48*(4), 918–925. https://doi.org/10.1016/j.jesp.2012.02.008

17 Ibid., page 919.

18 Frank, M. G., & Gilovich, T. (1988). The dark side of self- and social perception: Black uniforms and aggression in professional sports. *Journal of Personality and Social Psychology, 54*(1), 74–85. https://doi.org/10.1037/0022-3514.54.1.74

Chapter 8:

1 Wizards of the Coast (2014). *Dungeons & Dragons player's handbook.* Page 83.

2 Ibid., page 121.

3 Haidt, J. (2001). The emotional dog and its rational tail: A social intuitionist approach to moral judgment. *Psychological Review, 108*(4), 814–834. https://doi.org/10.1037/0033-295X.108.4.814

4 For this and the examples I give for other MFT dimensions, see Graham, J., Nosek, B. A., Haidt, J., Iyer, R., Koleva, S., & Ditto, P. H. (2011). Mapping the moral domain. *Journal of Personality and Social Psychology, 101*(2), 366–385. https://doi.org/10.1037/a0021847

5 For example, see Grizzard, M., & Ahn, C. (2017). Morality & personality: Perfect & deviant selves. In Banks, J. (Ed.), *Avatar, assembled: The social and technical anatomy of digital bodies* (pp. 117-126). https://doi.org/10.3726/978-1-4331-3829-4

6 Joeckel, S., Bowman, N. D., & Dogruel, L. (2012). Gut or game? The influence of moral intuitions on decisions in video games. *Media Psychology, 15*(4), 460–485. https://doi.org/10.1080/15213269.2012.727218

7 Tamborini, R., Bowman, N. D., Prabhu, S., Hahn, L., Klebig, B., Grall, C., & Novotny, E. (2018). The effect of moral intuitions on decisions in video game play: The impact of chronic and temporary intuition accessibility. *New Media and Society, 20*(2), 564–580. https://doi.org/10.1177/1461444816664356

8 Ibid., page 571.

9 I should note that there's nothing in the research that says real people can't be high on all the dimensions. Or low. Or anywhere between. But imposing these requirements on TTRPG characters makes things more interesting.

Chapter 9:

1 Hansley, K. (2020). "The gamble of Norway's King Olaf II for the island of Hising." *The History Hut.* https://thehistorianshut.com/2020/01/06/the-gamble-of-norways-king-olaf-ii-for-the-island-of-hising/ Retrieved October 8, 2021.

2 Aczel, A. (2005). *Chance: A guide to gambling, love, the stock market, and just about everything else.* Thunder Mouth Press.

3 Ladoucer, R., Paquet, C., & Dube, D. (1996). Erroneous perceptions in generating sequences of random events. *Journal of Applied Social Psychology, 2*(26), 2157–2166. https://doi.org/10.1111/j.1559-1816.1996.tb01793.x

4 Gilovich, T., Vallone, R., & Tversky, A. (1985). The hot hand in basketball: On the misperception of random sequences. *Cognitive Psychology, 17*(3), 295–314. https://doi.org/10.1016/0010-0285(85)90010-6

5 Oskarsson, A. T., Van Boven, L., McClelland, G. H., & Hastie, R. (2009). What's next? Judging sequences of binary events. *Psychological Bulletin, 135*(2), 262–285. https://doi.org/10.1037/a0014821

6 Braga, J. P. N., Mata, A., Ferreira, M. B., & Sherman, S. J. (2017). Motivated reasoning in the prediction of sports outcomes and the belief in the "hot hand." *Cognition and Emotion, 31*(8), 1571–1580. https://doi.org/10.1080/02699931.2016.1244045

7 Strickland, L. H, & Grote, F. W. (1967). Temporal presentation of winning symbols and slot machine playing. *Journal of Experimental Psychology, 74*(1), 10–13. https://doi.org/10.1037/h0024511

8 Parke, J., & Griffiths, M. (2004). Gambling addiction and the evolution of the "near miss." *Addiction Research and Theory, 12*(5), 407–411. https://doi.org/10.1080/16066350410001728118

9 Clark, L., Lawrence, A. J., Astley-Jones, F., & Gray, N. (2009). Gambling near-misses enhance motivation to gamble and recruit win-related brain circuitry. *Neuron, 61*(3), 481–490. https://doi.org/10.1016/j.neuron.2008.12.031

10 Amsel, A. (1958). The role of frustrative non reward in non continuous reward situations. *Psychological Bulletin, 55*, 102–119. https://doi.org/10.1037/h0043125

11 Henslin, J. (1967). Craps and magic. *American Journal of Sociology, 73*(3), 316–330. https://doi.org/10.1086/224479

12 Yee, N. (2013). *The Proteus paradox: How online games and virtual worlds change us-and how they don't.* Yale University Press.

13 Skinner, B. F. (1992). "Superstition" in the pigeon. 1948. *Journal of Experimental Psychology. General, 121*(3), 273–274. https://doi.org/10.1037/0096-3445.121.3.273

14 Yee, *The Proteus paradox.*

15 Fast, N. J., Gruenfeld, D. H., Sivanathan, N., & Galinsky, A. D. (2009). Illusory control. *Psychological Science, 20*(4), 502–508. https://doi.org/10.1111/j.1467-9280.2009.02311.x

Chapter 10:

1 For the sake of illustration, let's assume we're using the 2014 edition of the *Player's Handbook* to create your new character, plus some widely used options from *Xanathar's Guide to Everything* (2017) and *Tasha's Cauldron of Everything* (2020).

2 Iyengar, S. S., & Lepper, M. R. (2000). When choice is demotivating: Can one desire too much of a good thing? *Journal of Personality and Social Psychology, 79*(6), 995–1006. https://doi.org/10.1037//0022-3514.79.6.995

3 For more entertaining details on this jam study see chapter 6 in the main author's book: Iyengar, S. (2010). *The art of choosing.* Twelve.

4 Schwartz, B., Ward, A., Monterosso, J., Lyubomirsky, S., White, K., & Lehman, D. R. (2002). Maximizing versus satisficing: Happiness is a matter of choice.

Journal of Personality and Social Psychology, *83*(5), 1178–1197. https://doi.org/10.1037/0022-3514.83.5.1178

5 Tversky, A. (1972). Elimination by aspects: A theory of choice. *Psychological Review*, *79*(4), 281–299. https://doi.org/10.1037/h0032955

6 Hsee, C. K., & Zhang, J. (2004). Distinction bias: Misprediction and mischoice due to joint evaluation. *Journal of Personality and Social Psychology*, *86*(5), 680–695. https://doi.org/10.1037/0022-3514.86.5.680

7 Wilson, T. D., & Schooler, J. W. (1991). Thinking Too Much: Introspection can reduce the quality of preferences and decisions. *Journal of Personality and Social Psychology*, *60*(2), 181–192. https://doi.org/10.1037//0022-3514.60.2.181

8 Wilson, T. D., Lisle, D. J., Schooler, J. W., Hodges, S. D., Klaaren, K. J., & LaFleur, S. J. (1993). Introspecting about reasons can reduce post-choice satisfaction. *Personality and Social Psychology Bulletin*, *19*(3), 331–339. https://doi.org/10.1177/0146167293193010

9 This distinction in decision-making styles has been discussed widely, but it first appeared here: Simon, H. A. (1955). A behavioral model of rational choice. *Quarterly Journal of Economics*, *59*, 99-118. https://doi.org/10.2307/1884852

10 Iyengar, S. S., Wells, R. E., & Schwartz, B. (2006). Doing better but feeling worse: Looking for the "best" job undermines satisfaction. *Psychological Science*, *17*(2), 143–150. https://doi.org/10.1111/j.1467-9280.2006.01677.x

11 Gilbert, D. T., & Ebert, J. E. J. (2002). Decisions and revisions: The affective forecasting of changeable outcomes. *Journal of Personality and Social Psychology*, *82*(4), 503–514. https://doi.org/10.1037/0022-3514.82.4.503

12 Ibid., page 503.

Chapter 11:

1 Peterson, J. (2020). *The elusive shift: How role-playing games forged their identity*. MIT Press, page 40.

2 Rouse, W. B., & Morris, N. M. (1986). On looking into the black box: Prospects and limits in the search for mental models. *Psychological Bulletin*, *100*, 349–363. https://psycnet.apa.org/doi/10.1037/0033-2909.100.3.349

3 Cannon-Bowers, J. A., Salas, E., & Converse, S. A. (1993). Shared mental models in expert team decision making. In Castellan, N. J. (Ed.), *Individual and group decision making: current issues* (pp. 221–246). Erlbaum. https://doi.org/10.1037/12169-019

4 Waller, M. J., Gupta, N., & Giambatista, R. C. (2004). Effects of adaptive behaviors and shared mental models on control crew performance. *Management Science*, *50*(11), 1534–1544. https://doi.org/10.1287/mnsc.1040.0210

5 Mathieu, J. E., Heffner, T. S., Goodwin, G. F., Hobson, K., Ivory, K., Trip, M., & Windefelder, N. (2000). The influence of shared mental models on team process and performance. *Journal of Applied Psychology*, *85*(2), 273–283. https://doi.org/10.1287/mnsc.1040.0210

6 Lim, B. C., & Klein, K. J. (2006). Team mental models and team performance: A field study of the effects of team mental model similarity and accuracy. *Journal of Organizational Behavior*, *27*(4), 403–418. https://doi.org/10.1002/job.387

ENDNOTES

7 Geek & Sundry. (2016, July 6). *In the Belly of the Beast | Critical Role: Vox Machina | Episode 54* [Video]. YouTube. https://youtu.be/9QRg2YEkVLU

8 Osborn, A. F. (1957). *Applied imagination: Principles and procedures of creative problem solving*. Scribner.

9 Taylor, D. W., Berry, P. C., & Block, C. H. (1958). Does group participation when using brainstorming facilitate or inhibit creative thinking? *Administrative Science Quarterly, 3*, 23-47. https://psycnet.apa.org/doi/10.2307/2390603

10 Paulus, P. B., Putman, V. L., Dugosh, K. L., Dzindolet, M. T., & Coskun, H. (2002). Social and cognitive influences in group brainstorming: Predicting production gains and losses. *European Review of Social Psychology, 12*(1), 299–325. https://doi.org/10.1080/14792772143000094

11 Ibid.

12 Cooper, W. H., Gallupe, R. B., Pollard, S., & Cadsby, J. (1998). Some liberating effects of anonymous electronic brainstorming. *Small Group Research*, 29,147-78. https://psycnet.apa.org/doi/10.1177/1046496498292001

13 Paulus, P. B. & Kenworthy J. B. (2019). Effective brainstorming. In P. B. Paulus and B. A. Nijstad (Eds.) *Handbook of group creativity and innovation*. Oxford University Press.

14 Nijstad, B.A., & Stroebe, W. (2006). How the group affects the mind: A cognitive model of idea generation in groups. *Personality and Social Psychology Review, 10*(3), 186–213. https://doi.org/10.1207/s15327957pspr1003_1

15 Paulus & Kenworthy, *Effective brainstorming*.

16 Nemeth, C. J., Personnaz, B., Personnaz, M., & Goncalo, J. A. (2004). The liberating role of conflict in group creativity: A study in two countries. *European Journal of Social Psychology, 34*(4), 365–374. https://doi.org/10.1002/ejsp.210

17 Nemeth, C. J., & Ormiston, M. (2007). Creative idea generation: Harmony versus stimulation. *European Journal of Social Psychology, 37*(3), 524–535. https://doi.org/10.1002/ejsp.373

18 Duncker, K. (1945). On problem-solving (L. S. Lees, Trans.). *Psychological Monographs, 58*(5), i–113. https://doi.org/10.1037/h0093599

19 Kohn, N. W., Paulus, P. B., & Choi, Y. (2011). Building on the ideas of others: An examination of the idea combination process. *Journal of Experimental Social Psychology, 47*(3), 554–561. https://doi.org/10.1016/j.jesp.2011.01.004

Chapter 12:

1 The Mental Attic. (2014, May 5). Orr Group & Roll20.net [Blog post]. *The Mental Attic*. https://thementalattic.com/2014/05/05/orr-group-roll20-net/

2 Grouling, J. (2010). The unexpected responsibilities of managing an entire ecosystem: An interview with Roll20 creator Nolan T. Jones. In Hedge, S. & Gouling, J. (Eds.), *Roleplaying games in the digital age: Essays on transmedia storytelling, tabletop RPGs and fandom* (235-252). McFarland & Company.

3 ARLnow. (2015, July 27). Roll20 Creates Digital Game Table. *ARLnow*. https://www.arlnow.com/2015/07/27/roll20-creates-digital-game-table/

4 Wigglesworth, A. (2021, January 13). Online D&D provides relief amid COVID-19 pandemic. *Los Angeles Times*. https://www.latimes.com/california/story/2021-01-13/online-d-d-provides-relief-covid-19-pandemic

5 Ibid.

6 Ito, J. (2020, July 14). Roll20's userbase doubles as tabletop gaming shifts online. *Dicebreaker*. https://www.dicebreaker.com/companies/roll20/news/roll20-userbase-doubles

7 Kramer, A. (2021, March 13). Dungeons & Dragons had its biggest year ever, despite the coronavirus. *CNBC*. https://www.cnbc.com/2021/03/13/dungeons-dragons-had-its-biggest-year-despite-the-coronavirus.html

8 Bailenson, J. N. (2021). Nonverbal overload: A theoretical argument for the causes of Zoom fatigue. *Technology, Mind, and Behavior*, 2(1). https://doi.org/10.1037/tmb0000030

9 Bennett, A. A., Campion, E. D., Keeler, K. R., & Keener, S. K. (2021). Videoconference fatigue? Exploring changes in fatigue after videoconference meetings during COVID-19. *Journal of Applied Psychology*, 106(3), 330–344. https://doi.org/10.1037/apl0000906

10 Mehrabian, A. (1969). Some referents and measures of nonverbal behavior. *Behavioral Research Methods & Instruments*, 1(6), 203–207. https://psycnet.apa.org/doi/10.3758/BF03208096

11 Tomprou, M., Kim, Y. J., Chikersal, P., Woolley, A. W., & Dabbish, L. A. (2021). Speaking out of turn: How video conferencing reduces vocal synchrony and collective intelligence. *PLOS ONE*, 16(3), e0247655. https://doi.org/10.1371/journal.pone.0247655

12 Ibid.

13 Froming, W. J., Walker, G. R., & Lopyan, K.J. (1982). Public and private self-awareness: When personal attitudes conflict with societal expectations. *Journal of Experimental Social Psychology*, 18(5), 476-487. https://doi.org/10.1016/0022-1031(82)90067-1

14 Ratan, R., Miller, D. B., & Bailenson, J. N. (2022). Facial Appearance Dissatisfaction Explains Differences in Zoom Fatigue. *Cyberpsychology, Behavior, and Social Networking*, 25(2), 124–129. https://doi.org/10.1089/cyber.2021.0112

15 For example, listen to Dropbox. (Host). (2022, March 17). Faces [Audio podcast episode]. https://experience.dropbox.com/remotely-curious/faces

16 Weathermaster, T. (2024). Bwuahahaha! I'll show them, I'll show them all!. *Journal of Supervillain Monologues*, 44(2) 4-212.

17 Coleman, J. S. (1988). Social capital in the creation of human capital. *American Journal of Sociology*, 94, 95–120. https://doi.org/10.1086/228943

18 Kowert, R. (2020). "Social outcomes: online game play, social currency, and social ability." In Kowert, R & Quandt, T. (Eds.), *The Routledge handbook of digital media and communication* (pp. 87-98). Routledge.

19 Putnam R. (2000). *Bowling alone: The collapse and revival of American community*. Simon & Schuster.

20 Williams, D. (2007). The Impact of time online: Social capital and cyberbalkanization. *CyberPsychology & Behavior*, 10(3), 398–406. https://doi.org/10.1089/cpb.2006.9939

21 Galston, W. A. (2000). Does the internet strengthen community? *National Civic Review*, 89(3), 193–202. https://doi.org/10.1002/ncr.89302

ENDNOTES

22 Trepte, S., Reinecke, L., & Juechems, K. (2012). The social side of gaming: How playing online computer games creates online and offline social support. *Computers in Human Behavior, 28*(3), 832–839. https://doi.org/10.1016/j.chb.2011.12.003

23 Valkenburg, P. M., & Peter, J. (2009). Social consequences of the internet for adolescents: A decade of research. Current Directions in Psychological Science, *18*(1), 1-5. https://doi.org/10.1111/j.1467-8721.2009.01595.x

24 Kowert R., Oldmeadow J.A. (2013). (A)social reputation: Exploring the relationship between online video game involvement and social competence. *Computers In Human Behavior, 29*(4), 1872–1878. doi:10.1016/j.chb.2010.07.015

25 Scriven, P. (2021). From tabletop to screen: Playing Dungeons and Dragons during COVID-19. *Societies, 11*(4), 125 https://doi.org/10.3390/soc11040125

Chapter 13:

1 Ariely, D. (2010). The IKEA effect: why we overvalue what we make. In *The upside of irrationality: The unexpected benefits of defying logic at work and at home* (pp. 83–106). Harper Collins.

2 Norton, M., Mochon, D., & Ariely, D. (2012). The "IKEA effect": When labor leads to love. *Journal of Consumer Psychology, 22*(3), 453–460. https://psycnet.apa.org/doi/10.1016/j.jcps.2011.08.002

3 Festinger, L. (1957). *A theory of cognitive dissonance (Vol. 2)*. Stanford University Press.

4 Aronson, E., & Mills, J. (1959). The effect of severity of initiation on liking for a group. *The Journal of Abnormal and Social Psychology, 59*(2), 177-181. https://doi.org/10.1037/h0047195

5 Mochon, D., Norton, M. I., & Ariely, D. (2012). Bolstering and restoring feelings of competence via the IKEA effect. *International Journal of Research in Marketing, 29*(4), 363–369. https://doi.org/10.1016/j.ijresmar.2012.05.001

6 Marsh, L. E., Kanngiesser, P., & Hood, B. (2018). When and how does labour lead to love? The ontogeny and mechanisms of the IKEA effect. *Cognition, 170*, 245-253. https://doi.org/10.1016/j.cognition.2017.10.012

7 Peck, J., & Shu, S. B. (2009). The effect of mere touch on perceived ownership. *Journal of Consumer Research, 36*(3), 434-47. https://doi.org/10.1086/598614

8 Ariely, D. (2010). Paying more for less. In *The upside of irrationality: The unexpected benefits of defying logic at work and at home* (pp. 17–52). Harper Collins.

9 I'm not sure of the providence of this "name your monsters with characteristics starting with different letters" idea, but I first learned about it in an article by Mike "slyflourish" Shea at https://www.slyflourish.com.

10 Liu, W., & Gal, D. (2011). Bringing us together or driving us apart: The effect of soliciting consumer input on consumers' propensity to transact with an organization. *Journal of Consumer Research, 38*(2), 242–259. https://doi.org/10.1086/658884

Chapter 14:

1 de Kleer, E. (2017, July 24). *Dragons in the department of corrections*. Vice. https://www.vice.com/en/article/yvwnpx/dragons-in-the-department-of-corrections

2 Wilson, J. (2002, May). Trapped in real dungeons. *Dragon, 295,* 6-7.

3 Details about Singer's case discussed throughout this chapter were taken from the court's decision: Singer v. Raemisch, 611 F.3d 388 (7th Cir. 2010). I also offer a hat tip to Enworld.org forum user Michael Tresca for a pair of 2016 posts about escapism and TTRPGs in prisons.

4 Singer v. Raemisch, 611 F.3d 388 (7th Cir. 2010).

5 Baumeister, R. F. (1991). *Escaping the self: Alcoholism, spirituality, masochism, and other flights from the burden of selfhood.* Basic Books.

6 Kuss, D. J. (2013). Internet gaming addiction: Current perspectives. *Psychology Research and Behavior Management, 6,* 125–137. https://doi.org/10.2147/prbm.s39476

7 Stenseng, F., Falch-Madsen, J., & Hygen, B. W. (2021). Are there two types of escapism? Exploring a dualistic model of escapism in digital gaming and online streaming. *Psychology of Popular Media, 10*(3), 319–329. https://doi.org/10.1037/ppm0000339

8 Stenseng, F., Rise, J., & Kraft, P. (2012). Activity engagement as escape from self: The role of self-suppression and self-expansion. *Leisure Sciences, 34*(1), 19–38. https://doi.org/10.1080/01490400.2012.633849

9 Stenseng, Falch-Madsen, & Hygen. Are there two types of escapism?

10 Stenseng, Rise, & Kraft. Activity engagement as escape from self.

11 Stenseng, Falch-Madsen, & Hygen. Are there two types of escapism?

12 Giardina, A., Starcevic, V., King, D. L., Schimmenti, A., Di Blasi, M., & Billieux, J. (2021). Research directions in the study of gaming-related escapism: A commentary to Melodia, Canale, and Griffiths (2020). *International Journal of Mental Health and Addiction, 12,* 1075-1081. https://doi.org/10.1007/s11469-021-00642-8

13 Sonnentag, S., & Zijlstra, F. R. H. (2006). Job characteristics and off-job activities as predictors of need for recovery, well-being, and fatigue. *Journal of Applied Psychology, 91*(2). https://psycnet.apa.org/doi/10.1037/0021-9010.91.2.330

14 Collins, E., & Cox, A. L. (2014). Switch on to games: Can digital games aid post-work recovery? *International Journal of Human-Computer Studies, 72*(8–9), 654–662. https://doi.org/10.1016/j.ijhcs.2013.12.006

15 Sonnentag, S., & Bayer, U.V. (2005). Switching off mentally: Predictors and consequences of psychological detachment from work during off-job time. *Journal of Occupational Health Psychology, 10*(4), 393–414. https://doi.org/10.1037/1076-8998.10.4.393

16 Kubey, R. W., & Csikszentmihalyi, M. (1990). Television as escape: Subjective experience before an evening of heavy viewing. *Communication Reports, 3*(2), 92–100. https://doi.org/10.1080/08934219009367509

17 Reinecke, L. (2009). Games and recovery: The use of video and computer games to recuperate from stress and strain. *Journal of Media Psychology, 21*(3), 126–142. https://doi.org/10.1027/1864-1105.21.3.126

18 Collins, E., & Cox, A. L. (2014). Switch on to games: Can digital games aid post-work recovery? *International Journal of Human-Computer Studies, 72*(8–9), 654–662. https://doi.org/10.1016/j.ijhcs.2013.12.006

19 Reinecke. Games and recovery.

ENDNOTES

Chapter 16:

1 And that's just to play the game. I'm not even touching on how TTRPGs can be a springboard into other activities and skills like game design, video production, drawing, cartography, digital art, podcasting, miniature painting, and writing a book about the psychology of tabletop role-playing games.

2 Wizards of the Coast (2014). *Dungeons & Dragons Player's Handbook*, pg. 264.

3 Davis, A., & Johns, A. (2020). Dungeons, dragons, and social development. In Bean, A., Daniel, E., & Hays, S. (Eds.) *Integrating geek culture into therapeutic practice: The clinician's guide to geek therapy* (pp. 95-107). Leyline Publishing.

4 Kaylor, S. L. B. (2017). Dungeons and Dragons and literacy: The role tabletop role-playing games can play in developing teenagers' literacy skills and reading interests. *Graduate Research Papers, 215*. https://scholarworks.uni.edu/grp/215

5 Meriläinen, M. (2011). The self-perceived effects of the role-playing hobby on personal development – A survey report. *International Journal of Role Playing, 3*, 49–68. https://doi.org/10.33063/ijrp.vi3.224

6 Kilmer. E., Adam, D. Kilmer, J. & Johns, A. (2023). Case conceptualization and treatment planning in therapeutically applied role-playing games. In Kilmer. E., Adam, D., Kilmer, J., & Johns, A. (Eds.) *Therapeutically applied role-playing games: The Game to Grow method* (pp. 113-142). Routledge.

7 Connell, M., Kilmer, E., & Kilmer, J. (2020). Tabletop role playing games in therapy. In Bean, A., Daniel, E., & Hays, S. (Eds.) *Integrating geek culture into therapeutic practice: The clinician's guide to geek therapy* (pp. 75-93). Leyline Publishing.

8 Meriläinen. The self-perceived effects of the role-playing.

9 Kilmer et al. Case Conceptualization and Treatment Planning.

10 Driskell, J. E., Salas, E., & Driskell, T. (2018). Foundations of teamwork and collaboration. *American Psychologist, 73*(4), 334–348. https://doi.org/10.1037/amp0000241

11 Laal, M., Naseri, A. S., Laal, M., & Khattami-Kermanshahi, Z. (2013). What do we achieve from learning in collaboration? *Procedia - Social and Behavioral Sciences, 93*, 1427–1432. https://doi.org/10.1016/j.sbspro.2013.10.057

12 Kilmer et al. Case Conceptualization and Treatment Planning.

13 Moreno, J. D. (2014). *Impromptu man: J. L. Moreno and the origins of psychodrama, encounter culture, and the social network*. Bellevue Literary Press.

14 Bowman, S. L. & Lieberoth, A. (2018). Psychology and role-playing games. In Zagal, José P. and Deterding, S. (Eds.), *Role-playing game studies: Transmedia foundations*. Routledge (pp. 245-264).

15 Connell, M. (2023). *Tabletop role-playing therapy: A guide for the clinician game master*. W. W. Norton & Company.

16 Madigan, J. (2023, March 1). Therapy with Dungeons & Dragons (No. 82) [Audio podcast episode]. In The Psychology of Games Podcast. https://www.psychologyofgames.com/2023/03/podcast-82-therapy-with-dungeons-dragons/

17 Connell, M. (2023). Using tabletop role-playing games for specific diagnoses. In Connell, M. (Ed.) *Tabletop role-playing therapy: A guide for the clinician game master* (pp. 51-75). W. W. Norton & Company.

READY TO JOURNEY INTO THE

Checkpoints & Autosaves
By the time you reach the last page, you will have a guide to finding common ground with your child that will help you as a parent foster a better relationship, and maybe a new favorite hobby.

Final Fantasy
The Psychology of Final Fantasy guides gamers on a real-world quest of self-discovery so that they can surpass their own limit break.

Integrating Geek Culture
Integrating Geek Culture into Therapeutic Practice: The Clinician's Guide to Geek Therapy is a comprehensive compendium of how Geek Therapy clinicians and scholars currently use a variety of games, media artifacts, and other geek culture items in therapeutic context and intervention.

Geek Therapy Card Deck
The Geek Therapy Card Deck helps people find balance, reduce stress, bring awareness into their lives, and be mindful in the moment allowing them to manage distress, regulate their emotions and understand life relationships using Geek Cultural Artifacts and insights found within.

GEEK PSYCHOLOGY SERIES?

Meme Life
This book seeks to explain how memes influence societies and cultures.

Pokemon
The Psychology of Pokémon guides gamers on a real-world quest of self-discovery to unravel the mysteries of the Pokémon series.

Elden Ring
Few games have loomed as large in popular video game culture in recent years as Elden Ring, a devastatingly difficult sword-and-sorcery RPG that became a bestseller when it launched on PC, PlayStation, and Xbox consoles back in February 2022.

Visit our website for the full collection of Geek Psychology Series:
shop.geektherapeutics.com